The Smile File

The Precursors of Queen

C J Smith

AUREUS

First Published 2022
Digital Edition 2022
©2022   C J Smith
©2022   Digital Edition Chris Smith
©2022   Aureus Publishing Limited

Front cover: ©C J Smith and Meuryn Hughes
Widesmile Music Logo - ©River Six

Paperback ISBN : 978-1-899750-64-1
EPUB ISBN : 978-1-899750-65-8

Printed in Great Britain.
A catalogue record for this book is available from the British Library.
Aureus Publishing Limited
Tel: 00 44 (0) 1656 880033
E-mail: sales@aureus.co.uk
Web site: www.aureus.co.uk

Dedication: For three sisters – Laura, Emily and Zana

"It's tragic magic, there are no coincidences
but sometimes the pattern is more obvious."

(Keynsham by Neil Innes - The Bonzo Dog Doo-Dah Band)

Contents

Part One

Part Two

Part Three

Part One

1

The Headingley Cowboy

I was standing eating my ice cream, still holding the four-leaf clover, when the cowboy passed me on a horse. He was wearing a Stetson hat, neckerchief, checked shirt, guns and holsters, chaps and silver spurs. He pulled a toy cap gun out of his right holster, pointed it to the sky and squeezed the trigger. As the cap exploded overhead, he looked directly down at me from a tall horse, then, giving me a big wide Marlboro-Man grin, tipped his hat and said, "Howdie!" I looked on in awe as he rode off down the road firing his gun and then returned to my ice cream.

My mum shook her head and said something about him being a mad-man, but in my seven-year-old head, he was a western hero come to life. He'd jumped out of the TV or one of those cowboy films I'd seen at the Gaumont Cinema. In the 1950s, before rock n' roll, our heroes were cowboys; Roy Rodgers, Gene Autrey, Hop Along Cassidy, The Cisco Kid and Kit Carson, King of the Cowboys. Years later I found out that his wife had died and he'd gone a little crazy. To this day people still remember him as The Headingley Cowboy.

It had been the school sports day on Woodhouse Moor, not far from Leeds University, and that was the day I found out I could sprint. I had a crush on Susan Teale and she was watching, which might go some-way to account for my performance in the one hundred yards final. I came second.

My mum was sitting on the grass. I walked over feeling confused and sat down without saying a word. And that's when I found the four-leaf clover. Perhaps for doing well in the races or as a consolation, I don't know, she took me to Hyde Park Corner, not far from Headingley and bought me a Granelli's ice cream. That ice cream was the best I had ever tasted.

Some weeks later I would go with the school to watch my rival, the guy who'd pipped me at the post in the final race. He'd be representing the school on Children's Day and the inter-school Sports Day at Roundhay Park. Afterwards, as a final humiliation, he'd waltz off with my girl.

But right now, that hardly mattered, standing there on the pavement outside Granelli's. The sun was shining and this was my lucky day.

2

Buddy and Hank

Dev was leader of the pack. He wore a black jacket in place of the regulation blue school blazer. His deep red hair greased back into a perfect quiff with a DA (duck's arse) he was easily the coolest guy in school. At thirteen I thought myself lucky to be part of his gang, despite being lanky, spotty and still something of an outsider, especially when it came to sport. I could still sprint but anything over a hundred yards had me flagging. The other guys excelled at cross country running but, having asthma, I could hardly stagger down the road from the school gates without gasping for breath.

Dev showed up one day with an LP (long playing) record under his arm. Buddy Holly's songs were a revelation to me and spoke to teenagers all over the country from Liverpool to London. I'd missed Elvis (too young I guess) but Buddy seemed more real somehow. He was downright gawky, had a certain vulnerability and yet was charismatic. He hadn't just stepped out of a mould like Billy Fury or Elvis. You sensed he might have suffered from pimples at some time, if not terminal acne. His songs gave the impression he knew the problems of actually getting round to talking to girls, especially the very pretty middle-class girls from Bramhope like Greta Pickup and Marilyn Butcher.

Then here come The Shadows, a boys' band. Cliff was strictly for the girls, but The Shads; you'd never heard anything like the twang of Hank Marvin's Stratocaster. Thankfully, Hank was another gawky Buddy Holly lookalike with the same glasses, only from nearer home. And then there were those Fender guitars we could only dream of possessing; Hank's fiesta-red, maple-necked Strat, Bruce Welsh's white Telecaster with a rosewood fingerboard and Jet Harris's three tone sunburst Precision bass.

There was another reason, apart from the love of music, why nerdy guys took up the guitar and previously painfully shy boys were suddenly inspired to become exhibitionist lead singers; imagine going to a dance where the boys are lined up on one side of the dancehall facing the girls lined up on the other. As a boy, you now have the humiliating task of crossing that no-man's land to ask a girl to dance, the chances of rejection, astronomical. Following the expected rebuff, there are two choices; the first, a mortifying return across no- man's land to the trenches. The second choice, even worse, asking the girl sitting to the left of your intended conquest, who, if she possesses an ounce of self-respect, will have to tell you to just fuck off.

You can see it's all stacked against you, just as it's stacked against the girls but then suddenly you glimpse a way out of this embarrassing predicament.

You notice those guys on the stage are suddenly the focal point of the entire room as soon as they get up to play their guitars and drums. They are exempt from the humiliating ritual and the dancing and now, girls are extremely interested in them.

I don't know how I got there, who I was with or who the group was, but I still have this vision; I was standing on the balcony at the King's Hall, Ilkley, and down below me, people were dancing. Up on the stage three guitarists were standing on circular rostrums elevating them high above the crowd. They were all wearing matching blue suits with velvet collars, sporting Tony Curtis haircuts and playing red guitars. Behind them the drummer had taken his suit jacket off. He was playing like the devil on a red sparkle drum kit and under the blue stage lights the atmosphere was electric. With every twang of those silver strings and every aching bend of the whammy-bar those Fender guitars spoke of desire and all I remember thinking was, I want to do that. Soon there must have been at least twenty groups (we called them groups in those days) playing Shadows numbers in the local area.

I bought my first EP (extended play, with two tracks on each side) Spotlight on the Shadows and then a few weeks later my second EP, Shadows to the Four and played them continuously on my Dansette record player. You could stack up the singles and EPs on a metal rod to play one after the another. But the best place to hear them was at the Beech Hill Picture House, which had those massive speakers. Hearing the Shadows as they were meant to be heard had a profound impact.

I wanted desperately to make that sound. I just had to have a guitar. I slowly came to the realisation that I was making new friends who felt exactly the same way about this new music that our parents couldn't understand. Apache, Midnight, Peace Pipe, The Savage, FBI; these titles conjured up fantastic images but it was Wonderful Land, with full orchestra, that for the newly initiated became a mystical experience.

I was lighting up my first Woodbine in the Toblerone dark of that Kia-Ora dawn. I was a thirteen-year-old kid. I was solid gone and I was never coming back.

3

The Ladykillers

After school we'd stand in the bus station to see Geoff, the lead guitarist of The Senators, arriving from Harrogate Art College. Geoff had hair down to his waist like Phil May of the Pretty Things. You couldn't miss him.

Johnny Vincent would go round to Geoff's house for guitar lessons. Every time Geoff went out of the room, Johnny would pick up his cherry red Gibson 335 and do a quick pose in the mirror. He'd be careful to put the guitar back exactly where he found it before our hero returned.

I went to see The Senators play a barn dance at a local farm. We sat on bales of hay smoking cigarettes and trying not to set the place on fire. Des O'Hara's bass bounced off the walls and came up through the floor. I recall

1965, The Ladykillers with their 1934 Rolls-Royce hearse.
L-R; Mick Larvin, Barry Clements, Des O'Hara, Andy Moss and Geoff Chew

the physical sensation, the excitement of feeling it through my feet. The Senators were a few years older than us. We'd salivate over the Gibson and Gretsch guitars they played, plugged into Vox AC30s and Fender amps. These were the big boys and in 1965 they changed their name to The Ladykillers.

Andy Moss, their rhythm guitarist, had dyed his hair blond but it came out pink. He was clearly seen driving around town in a huge 1934 Rolls Royce hearse with a sign announcing The Ladykillers, the car covered in affectionate messages written in lipstick. (We were never sure whether the authors were genuine female fans or The Ladykillers themselves.) In a small Yorkshire market town like Otley in the mid-sixties, the hearse caused apoplectic outrage among some of the more prominent members of the religious community. I didn't know it yet but I'd be seeing more of Andy Moss and Des O'Hara in a later incarnation. The times certainly were a-changing.

4

The Bulldogs

M y initiation to beat groups was purely accidental. In 1960 I was a keen boy scout and the Bulldog Patrol's task for that month was to form a skiffle group. The Patrol's second in command did a tolerable Lonny Donegan impersonation, singing through his teeth. If you half closed your eyes, he did indeed look a bit like Lonny himself.

As Billy Bragg pointed out in his book, Roots, Radicals and Rockers (How Skiffle Changed the World), [1] it was a D.I.Y movement. All you needed was a cheap guitar, three chords, a tea-chest bass and a washboard. You didn't have to be a musician and when we heard Lonnie Donegan singing Lead-belly's Rock Island Line it was a rallying cry for thousands of teenage boys to form Skiffle groups. It undermined the music business; those staid middle-aged Tin-Pan Alley guys didn't know what hit them. This was a purely British phenomenon and the beginning of a youth revolution that evolved into rock and roll. This revolution began in back-rooms, youth clubs, church halls and scout huts up and down Britain. Like the punk revolution in the seventies, these returns to primitive music making are healthy. Kids who would have been put off by the thought of having to learn to read music are suddenly free to express themselves and fired up about making a bedlam of adolescent noise.

My task was to build a tea-chest bass, complete with broom handle and a piece of string. The tea-chest acted as a crude amplifier. Theoretically you change the pitch by tightening the string with the broom handle. In fact, altering the pitch in a controllable way is almost impossible and at best it gives off a dull thud, (although I'm sure there are some clever and dedicated players who have mastered the intricacies of pitch control.)

Still, the Bulldogs' Skiffle Group managed a fair rendition of Cumberland Gap. I gave a spirited and energetic performance, throwing myself so thoroughly into the part, that 'Lonny' promptly asked me to play bass guitar in his beat group, the Blue Sapphires.

I didn't know one end of a bass from the other. Full of optimism I borrowed my friend Brian Duffersey's Rosetti bass and, with no rehearsal whatsoever, set off to perform at Burley Social Club.

The house lights dimmed. The large youth club audience, now crowding around the front of the stage, suddenly became hushed.

One solitary blue spotlight shone on Geoff Hollins' blue sparkle drum kit. I stood to Geoff's right at the back like a rabbit in the headlights, trying to give the illusion that I had at least a clue what I was doing.

'Lonny' turned up his Watkins Copicat echo unit and strummed an arpeggio. Geoff's drums started quietly at first on the bass tom-tom, then grew louder and suddenly we were off into Billy Fury's It's Only Make Believe.

The singer stepped up to the microphone. He had those big Jagger lips, was extremely overweight, and a string vest could be clearly seen grinning through his Nylon shirt. He was wearing huge grey flannel trousers you could have easily rented out to a family of share croppers. He completed this remarkable combination with a pair of Tuff sensible shoes. I can't say it was a good look but what he lacked in style, he more than made up for with his performance. Down on one knee, microphone held high and tilted downwards, he stared into the blue spotlight with tears in his eyes and, like Johnny Ray, gave it his all. Meanwhile, for me, at the back of the stage, it was panic stations. I thought it best to play safe and stick to playing the bottom E string.

Following this performance, the group split owing to 'musical differences.' Lonnie and Mick were gone, leaving Geoff and I to pursue a bright future with endless possibilities of fame and fortune in the dazzling world of rock n' roll.

5

Sex Education

Of course, we were never told anything. What I learned in the school yard, at first seemed about as implausible as my parents' religious beliefs. Most parents avoided the sex talk; however, my friend David Hudson's mother was obviously more enlightened.

To Dave's utter horror she took him into the kitchen and told him to sit down. "I think it's time we had a little talk, David."

Dave stared at the floor, buttocks firmly clenched.

She went on, "You know how your sister's starting to grow hair under her arms?"

"Yes......"

"Well, in a year or two you'll get hair growing under your arms too."

And that was it.

6

Out of The Shadows

That Saturday morning I'd caught the bus into Leeds. Going into the record department at Barker's on the Headrow was an exciting new world. I was thirteen. I made my request at the counter and the assistant pointed towards the record booths along the far wall. Booth number three was where my request would be played. This was all new to me but soon the twang of Hank Marvin's guitar transported me in my imagination to realms only a Fender Stratocaster could travel. Mark Knopfler said he remembers the smell of the Fender guitar catalogue. You could only dream of owning a Fender like Hank's - they were impossibly expensive.

I paid for the record and left the shop with my treasured purchase.

In England, coffee-bars were cool places where teenagers went to "hang out" like in American films. I ordered my frothy coffee, found an empty window seat and stared at the record cover. There they were, The Shad's; four black silhouettes in a yellow spotlight, against a black background. In red letters, against the yellow spotlight, it read Spotlight on The Shadows. I turned it over and there were the four titles, The Frightened City, Kon-tiki, Peace Pipe and The Savage. I took the record out of its sleeve. I could smell the vinyl. It had a black label which said COLUMBIA in blue letters. Under a blue circle containing two black semi-quavers, in silver, it read 45 RPM and under that EXTENDED PLAY.

My parents had a Radiogram, a piece of furniture which combined a radio and a record player, mainly used by my mother to play the sound-tracks from musicals, which she loved. She had an old 78 of Nymphs and Shepherds (which I loathed because it was simply dreadful). She also had several 78s of a big band, whose leader, Ambrose, (!) she'd probably had a crush on in her teens. For all her appalling musical taste, she still managed to voice her disapproval of anything with drums and guitars, a prejudice which remained firmly entrenched.

On Saturday mornings, having made a few quid from my paper round, I'd take the bus and head for Barker's record department, then I'd head back to the coffee-bar. The first LP I bought was The Buddy Holly Story. Those moments, mulling over my new record, sipping my frothy coffee, I'd instantly be transported to rock and roll heaven. There I could forget the anxieties and insecurities of my early teens. Forget about having to pretend I'd been paying attention in class, when really, I was far too busy dreaming about guitars and girls.

In rock and roll heaven, for just a few precious minutes, those problems with my parents, those feelings of not belonging, were vanquished.

7

With the Beatles

She was big, brash and loud and always got top marks in art. She was frankly scary and, at fourteen, not the kind of girl I'd normally dare to go anywhere near. Despite terminal acne and crippling shyness on my part we seemed to bond over art and pop music. Linda Williams bounced over to my desk after French brandishing a picture of a new band. There were just four heads minus the standard slicked back hair. These guys looked different, looked cool, even with their pudding basin haircuts.

Three looked relatively unremarkable, but one face stood out. This guy looked tough. There was a lot in that face; he certainly wasn't ordinary. I stared at that face, shocked, like I was looking into the face of Jesus. I hadn't even heard their music but I had to find out more.

The Beatles arrived at the start of the sixties, which for us baby boomers coincided with the onset of puberty, a condition widely unacknowledged by our parents, the church or the rest of society. From the age of thirteen, my parents didn't recognise me and I felt increasingly exiled from who they thought I was. All that religious guilt and sexual repression was a time bomb waiting to explode.

And here come the Beatles, "One two three four, well she was just seventeen, you know what I mean," [1] and, yes, we knew exactly what they meant. They were northerners, cheeky and funny and they reminded you of yourself and your mates. At last, someone was talking our language. Until now, love and sex had been a sin, and now at last, it was something to be celebrated. I can't overstate what a breath of fresh air The Beatles were. They were more than a band for us, they were a miracle. They blew the lid off all that terrible repression and invited us to come along and have some fun at last.

In his book, Chronicles, Bob Dylan said, "The Beatles offered intimacy and companionship like no other group". [2]

Like James Dean and Marlon Brando, Lennon clearly represented the rebel, the outsider; "What are you rebelling against, Johnny?" [3] John was the brother you never had, brave and fearless and, like George Harrison said, you would have followed him into a war zone. In common with many teenagers that Christmas of '63, I drove my parents crazy continuously playing With the Beatles. I'd be trying to work out who was playing what, absorbing the songs and harmonies.

I needed a proper electric guitar. Badly.

8

FO Guitar

Twist and Shout would be my vocal debut. It was the Boy Scouts' Gang Show and Roy Hendry and I were forming a beat group for two performances. Hastily recruiting Robert Tindle on bass and Phil Atkinson to play drums, we were allotted a short slot for two songs. Roy would play rhythm guitar because he knew more chords than me. I would play lead guitar, which was a way around the little-known fact that I still hadn't mastered the difficult bar chord. I bluffed my way through the rehearsals by playing only one note at a time.

Roy had his own guitar, a brand-new Hofner Futurama. I'd borrowed a red Hofner Colorama with a black scratch plate from my friend, Trevor Platt, of The Patriots.

Trevor lived down the road from me and The Patriots rehearsed at his house. He played lead guitar while my friend, Derek Cheetham, played rhythm guitar. Derek and I had both joined the Parish Church choir the same week. Derek was The Patriots' lead singer, played left-handed and had a white Strat years before Jimi Hendrix. Chris Gravel was an extremely musical bass player; he could play the Jet Harris bass solo from Nivram, (Marvin spelt backwards) perfectly, so we knew he was good. John Mason held his drumsticks correctly so we were confident he must be an accomplished drummer. It was the first time I'd spent any time with a beat group and they invited me to sit in on an Animals' song for which they needed a keyboard player. I learned technical stuff from The Patriots, about guitars and amps, as well as how a band works putting the music together. All of this proved useful when it came to rehearsing my vocal debut at the Boy Scouts' Gang Show.

The Gang Show was at what was previously the Burras Lane School Rooms. It was now the Church Hall where I attended the church youth club. We opened with the instrumental FBI by the Shadows and then the big finish, Twist and Shout. I took my cue from the newly released Beatles version, with my best attempt to sound like John, old leather-lungs himself.

Surprisingly the gig was a great success and I even managed to get my Beatle jacket torn by a fan, (her name was Ruth). I'd borrowed the jacket as

Vocal debut, Twist and Shout; Boy Scout's Gang Show

well, and had to have it invisibly mended before returning it.

Roy now hinted that it was time I bought my own electric guitar. He suggested that I buy an FO guitar. My mum agreed to help and we duly arrived at Alan and Walker's music shop in Ilkley. The shop owner was clearly puzzled when I requested an FO guitar, then suddenly dissolved into laughter on realising it was an f hole guitar I was after. (The sound holes are f-shaped, hence the name.) Sounding your H's was considered 'soft' if you were a schoolboy in Otley in those days and Roy was no exception to the rule.

We left the shop with an FO guitar, an Egmond acoustic, and it was a dog but I didn't realise that at the time. It wasn't even electric but the shopkeeper managed to persuade us to buy a cheap pickup. The guitar was green to black sunburst and you could have driven a bus under the twelfth fret. These guitars were cheese graters, and the strength required to hold down a string (let alone a chord) was Herculean. Consequently, considerable dedication was required, resulting in shredded and bleeding fingers.

A friend, who visited Shearer's music shop in Leeds, tried out a top of the range Gibson semi acoustic. It played so easily he thought it was specially designed for people with disabilities.

I did eventually master the bar chord and progressed to better guitars. But for ever after that, whenever the word guitar was mentioned in our house, my mother would ask, "Is it an FO guitar?"

9

Square Neck

"**S**hort back 'n' sides sir?" Wood's was the army barber; he only did short back 'n' sides. The other was Tom's, the Teds' barber. I dreamed of becoming a Teddy Boy but there was no chance. Tom Ramsden could do you a cool 'Tony Curtis' with a spectacular quiff and DA, but sadly, in my case, it was not to be. I was sent to Wood's. Mr Wood, however, not to be entirely consigned to the outposts of hair styling, branched out by adding an alternative, the Square Neck, to his tonsorial vocabulary.

I went home with my collar turned up and my father was most disapproving. Mr Wood, flushed with success, branched out yet again and introduced the Flattop. (Where would this coiffeur's innovations ever end?)

To my amazement my dad approved of the flattop, saying I looked like an American GI.

Eventually I did get up the nerve to go to Tom's. When I sat in the chair, I couldn't help noticing the sink in front of me held a mountain of Durex. Some of the old men had singes. Tom would set their hair on fire at the back with a taper. What was that about? It smelt terrible.

Anything for the weekend sir?

10

All the Fun of the Fair

As far back as I remember, the end of summer was time for the Woodhouse Feast and, on the fairground at Hyde Park Corner, the Ferris wheel, the waltzer and the ghost train would arrive. Everything was steam driven in those days by hissing, oily, pulsating engines. There were steam swings, big cages where you had to hang on to the bars for dear life. There were no safety belts; you took your life in your hands. There was a freak show with a five- legged sheep and strange things preserved in glass jars, like Siamese twins. Young men tried to impress their girlfriends on the Test Your Strength machine where you brought down a big hammer. If you managed to sound the bell right at the top of the score-board, you were the champ. There was a shooting gallery, candyfloss, toffee-apples, Hook-a-Duck and kiddies rides. It was an annual outing for all the family.

In my teens, when the fair came to Otley, I remember the Teddy-boys standing around the waltzer, with girls who looked like Amy Winehouse or The Ronettes. Their world seemed impenetrable, dangerous and extremely glamorous.

The Teds who worked on the ride would jump on and spin you, then jump off at great risk to life and limb. What I do remember are the hits of the day, played at maximum volume. The sound fading and then returning as you went around. The Clapping Song; "The line broke, the monkey got choked and they all went to heaven in a little row-boat." [1] The Kinks' You Really Got Me - "I believe that you and me last for ever." 2 Leader of the Pack or Jerry Lee Lewis singing Chantilly Lace. It said "Hi kid, welcome to the greasy end of rock'n'roll."

11

The Vox

Ibought the Vox guitar from Allan Pyrah (who would figure significantly later in my musical life). The guitar was finished in plain wood, a small bodied electric with one cutaway. It cost me seven pounds if I remember correctly. They currently can sell for over three grand. It had a long headstock with all six machine heads running along the top like on a Fender Strat. It was a copy of a Japanese guitar, played by Hank Mervin, (the Guyatone/ Antoria LG50). I stood it by my bed so it would be the first thing I'd see when I woke up. Not being able to afford an amp was a problem. I'd sit in the bathroom with the guitar headstock pressed against the side of the bath, which amplified the sound a little. Eventually I did manage to buy a cheap amp. I'd carry the guitar and amp to Geoff Hollins' house off Weston Lane to practise. I bought the Big Three EP, Live at the Cavern, and studied Brian Griffiths' guitar licks. He played a Hofner Colorama, like the one I'd borrowed from my friend Trevor Platt of The Patriots.

Occasionally Ginner Bramley would bring his guitar, a red Watkins Rapier, over to Geoff's house and one night a guy called Buzzer Ives turned up with a Hofner President. To us it seemed like a top of the range Gibson. It looked expensive. We were just learning, but for Geoff and myself, this was going to be a lifetime obsession.

Learning Beatles' songs was a good way to learn new guitar chords because they used all the regular chords but also included one or two chords you didn't know. The Beatles didn't read music and were primitive musicians like most of us so it's likely they'd only just discovered those new chords themselves. They'd started with Buddy Holly and three chords and developed from there.

The Big Three was the biggest group in Liverpool for a while. I remember a poster where they headlined, with the Beatles at the bottom of the bill. Their EP, Live at the Cavern, still sounds amazing today.

Before Brian Griffiths joined, their guitarist was Adrian Barber. Adrian was from Otley and in those days his family had a tobacconist's shop on the high street. (His cousin, Lynne Barber, who taught English at my school, was extremely cool and dressed like a beatnik. Some of us fifth formers were invited over to her house one Sunday for afternoon tea and I felt very honoured that she had included me among the cool kids.)

Adrian built a massive bass cabinet for Johnny Gustafson, the Big Three's bass player, which became known as the Coffin.[1] He subsequently built Coffin bass cabs for Paul McCartney, and installed a similar bass cab at the Star Club in Hamburg, where he was stage manager for eighteen months. It was powered by one of the clubs' cream coloured Fender Bassman amps and Paul used this while John and George played through the club's cream Fender Bandmaster "piggy-back" amps. (My wife, Jane, tells me she's just glazed over but I insist, there are gear-nerds out there like myself who will be fascinated by this stuff.) On the Beatles' last visit to the Star Club, this time with Ringo, Adrian recorded them and his recordings were released fifteen years later as the album, Beatles Live! At The Star Club Germany, 1962.

John Lennon said, "You should have been there." Adrian Barber was.

Johnny Gustafson later joined The Merseybeats and in the early seventies, my band, Big Black Sedan, played a gig supporting his band, Bullet. Following the gig, I found Johnny sitting on his own in the dressing room. He rolled us a joint and, as we smoked it, I finally got a chance to tell him how much that Big Three record meant to me.

12

The Cavern Club

We were standing directly over the stage, on the wooden cover that had once been the cellar's loading bay. That evening the club was about to open and the group were finishing their sound check. At one point I was standing directly above the bass player's amp and I could feel the vibrations of those bass notes up through my feet.

It was the summer of '64 and I was going on holiday with my folks to North Wales. We were going with the Atkinsons, Fred and Phyllis, their daughter Lucy who was a couple of years older than me and their son Philip. Phil was a friend from school and had played drums in our first band at the Boy Scout's Gang Show. The two of us cooked up a plan.

Queuing outside the Cavern Club

To reach North Wales in those days, the quickest way was through the Mersey Tunnel. In 1964 Liverpool was a Mecca for teenage music fans and we certainly were not going to miss the opportunity to visit the Cavern Club.

Lucy, Phil and I made our way to Matthew Street where a long queue had already formed. We had been queuing outside the Grapes and I'd noticed a television crew and a big BBC camera parked by the club's entrance. By now the doors were open and the excited crowd was slowly making its way down the stone steps into the holy of holies. I noticed the camera swing round till I was clearly in its sights. In my excitement and with an involuntary movement, I peered over the head of the crowd and mouthed, "Hello!" at the camera.

At the bottom of the stone steps, we paid our entrance fee and collected our tickets. Inside, the stone walls were dripping with condensation. We had no idea who the band was going to be that night. It turned out to be Herman's Hermits from Manchester. They had a record in the charts called I'm Into Something Good, a chirpy little pop song I'd heard on the radio and liked. It turned out it was written by Goffin and King. I noticed the Hermit's bass player played left-handed like Paul McCartney. In a dark corner over by the wall, was a real mean looking fella. He looked like a merchant seaman and he had a knife up against somebody's throat. I thought to myself, this is a more dangerous place than I'd anticipated. There was only the one way in and out of there.

In another year or so I'd be playing in cellar dives and places like this all over the north of England. As the three of us surfaced again into Matthew Street, to re-join our parents and head to Wales, my head was buzzing.

I felt like I'd been to the centre of the earth.

Many years later I was watching a video with a shot of a crowd queuing outside the Cavern Club. I noticed this kid push his head up above the crowd, and mouth, "Hello!" I thought, that kid looks a lot like I used to look in those days.

I re-wound the video. I thought, he's even wearing a jacket very much like the one I used to have,

I re-wound the video again. I thought, the way his hair is slicked back is just the way I used to have mine.

On the third rewind the penny dropped.

It turns out this is the only footage of a crowd outside the Cavern. So far, I've appeared in films about Johnny Kidd and the Pirates, Cilla Black, John Lennon and most documentaries featuring the Cavern Club.

It turned out to be my first TV appearance. Look out for me; I'm the spotty sixteen-year-old bobbing his head up and saying, "Hello!"

13

Church

F red Mason, the choirmaster, would sit directly behind us during the sermon. If we talked, he would rap us very hard on the top of our heads with his knuckles. Dave Hudson, Derek Cheetham and I had all joined the Parish Church choir at the age of nine in the same week. We were still probationers so wore the purple cassock, still minus the regulation ruffle and surplus. Photographs of me in full regalia which my mother proudly displayed on her mantlepiece, having dragged me reluctantly to a local photographer, would be the cause excruciating embarrassment. I eventually destroyed the evidence.

I'd recently moved from Leeds to Otley, from an inner city to a small market town. I found I had to address the school mistress as Ma'am instead

of Miss, and I had to learn to write in italics. It all seemed very quaint and unreal. I soon became bored and lost interest in schoolwork. With practice I learned to feign interest while in my imagination I was off on my bike down the river somewhere. I soon became a country boy and grew to love living in Otley. I felt like Huckleberry Finn.

Though schoolwork had become a drag, music was different. Apart from the comradery of being in the choir, I loved the harmony singing and was thrilled by the grandeur of the sound it produced. When Fred Mason retired, Kenneth Alway took over. He was an eccentric young man in his early thirties with a terrific sense of humour. He soon spotted that I had a good soprano voice and suggested I learn the piano as it would give me a grounding in music. It was the best advice anyone could have given me and I'm eternally grateful to him and so, he became my piano teacher.

He had a teddy bear called the Earl of Drumnadrochit who played the bagpipes. The bear would whisper in his ear (presumably in a broad Scottish accent) and he would translate for me. This would include endless furious complaints and swearing, much to my delight.

After the war there had been shortages and rationing. It was Harvest Festival and there were no bananas, so for the organ voluntary he'd played a thinly disguised version of Yes, We Have No Bananas. Sadly, after a couple of years he left for a job as music teacher at Scarborough College.

The Earl of Drumnadrochit

Godfrey Turner, who took over as organist and choirmaster, and later as my piano teacher, was very different. A dour Bradfordian, with absolutely no sense of humour, who smoked a pipe, yet he was an accomplished musician with an assortment of letters after his name. The comedian, Billy Connelly, said, "Never trust a man who, when left alone in a room with a tea-cosy, doesn't try it on his head." That's the difference between my two piano teachers; Mr Alway would definitely have tried on the tea-cosy.

On becoming a teenager, as I discovered rock and roll and grew bored of practicing the piano for forty minutes every day. I dutifully completed the piano practice just so I could play my guitar (or 'that damned guitar' as it was commonly known in our house). Mr Turner noted my lack of interest in the piano and suggested I take some lessons on the church organ.

I took to it straight away, particularly becoming fascinated with Bach's Preludes and Fugues. By the age of seventeen I was performing solo organ recitals at the church. Previously, before my voice broke, Mr Turner had honed my solo singing and encouraged me to enter singing competitions. He would drill me to smooth out my Yorkshire accent and perfect my phrasing.

Shortly after my Confirmation and just as my voice was about to break, I lost my faith. (Actually, I didn't feel I'd lost anything, so much as gained enlightenment.) I stopped saying the creed and the curate complained to my parents that, as head boy, I was setting a bad example to the other choirboys, but by this time my interests were elsewhere.

The church provided a valuable musical education for many rock musicians including harmony, musical structure and form. I was fully aware that there was a renaissance happening, but this time it wasn't in religious music.

14

A Picture of Jesus

The vestry door had a huge iron key which I had to collect from the verger, John Peel. I'd generally find him at the Whitakers Arms. John enjoyed a drink and on Sunday mornings, tended to totter slightly as he led the vicar to the pulpit. Turning the key in the heavily studded black door, then locking it behind me, I'd walk through the dimly lit vestry into the silent church. I'd press the button to switch on the machinery that would start up the mighty pipe organ. Deep groans and sighs would exude from the ancient mechanism. You could imagine a colony of bats taking flight from the clock tower, clouds of dust, clocks that hadn't chimed for millennia suddenly restored to life.

A mirror was situated over the organ console so that the organist could

see the choir during the services. There was a light over the mirror, otherwise the church was in darkness, save for a small spotlight over the altar. I'd soon be lost in the sounds and complexities of a Bach fugue. His music has a hypnotic effect on me, not too dissimilar from the effect that Skip James or John Lee Hooker's blues would have in future years. After an hour's rehearsal, I'd once again unlock the heavily studded black door, lock it behind me, fight my way through the smoke-filled bar at the Whitakers and return the key to John Peel.

As if going into the church alone wasn't scary enough for my teenage imagination, there was a painting of Jesus that I had to pass each time. It hung on the wall next to the altar. Jesus had his eyes closed but it was cleverly painted in such a way that, when you looked at it for a few moments, the eyes appeared to open. Seated alone at the organ in the solemn darkness of the church, I would imagine, if I turned around, or looked in the mirror, he might be standing right behind me and I'd die of fright.

15

The Flicks

"We're off to t'flicks."After the war, before television, most people went to the cinema. There were cinemas everywhere in Leeds. Our local cinema was the Hyde Park Picture House and it's still there today, preserved as it always was and now run by dedicated volunteers. The Cottage Road Cinema in Headingley is similarly preserved in aspic but most of those old Flea pits are gone today.

My cousin Christine, who's five years older than me, remembers taking me as a small boy to the Gaumont in City Square, where they showed Popeye, Mickey Mouse and Bugs Bunny cartoons. I remember The Three Stooges and Westerns like The Lone Ranger.

Later when I saw my first feature films, they were so powerful they fuelled my imagination. At school my drawings and paintings were filled with a combination of characters from the different films that obsessed my every waking minute. There could be, for instance, a coastal scene with tall cliffs. On top of the cliffs would be the Alamo with Davy Crocket fighting off the Mexican army, soldiers in blue coats, climbing ladders to scale the walls. Below the cliffs was the Nautilus from 20000 Leagues Under the Sea and further out at sea sailed The Pequod, being rammed by Moby Dick with Captain Ahab hitching a ride. Rob Roy would be in there too, up on a hill somewhere with the Redcoats chasing him. Over there was King Arthur and The Knights of the Round Table and docked down in the bay, a Viking longship. Nearby, on a high castle wall, you could see Kirk Douglas and Tony Curtis having a sword-fight to the death. It seemed only right to have them all in the same picture just as they were all living constantly in my head.

When I moved with my mum and dad to Otley at the age of nine, there were two cinemas, the Kirkgate Cinema and the Beech Hill Picture House. It was some friend's birthday and, instead of a party, us kids were taken to the Kirkgate Cinema to see The Duke Wore Jeans, featuring Tommy Steel. It wasn't a great film but it did make me aware of Tommy Steel and consequently, I eventually found my way to rock and roll. And then to my delight, I discovered Little Richard, Jerry Lee Lewis and the Everly Brothers.

After choir practice on Friday evenings, some of us choirboys would go across the road from the church and round to the back door of the Kirkgate Cinema. There was a hole, about an inch in diameter, in the door, providing a full view of the cinema screen if you pressed your eye against it. We'd watch X-rated horror films, taking it in turns and stare in fear and awe at the sheer terror. I remember seeing most of It; The Monster from Beyond Space, before being shouted at by the projectionist, who would occasionally come out and rattle the dustbins, yelling at us to "Clear off!"

The reason cinema became so significant for me is that it drew me towards cinematic songs. For instance, Dylan's songs are filled with visual imagery. There are some who claim that opera is the most profound art form, some would say it's cinema but I've come to believe that it's song-writing.

Take Dylan's song, Simple Twist of Fate, for example; there's that little green park with the girl on the park bench. When Bob Dylan wrote that song, I might be wrong but I would venture to suggest he had his own picture of a park and a certain young woman in mind. When we hear the song, we project our own lives into the song. There's our own little green park and our own personal memory of a young woman. It could be just a dream of what might happen in the future or more likely, the song awoke feelings of love you had for that particular person. The fact is, you inhabited Dylan's song with your own life, your own emotions and he provided a framework for you to do that. To me, that is truly profound and it is a kind of magic.

16

Stones in my Pathway

In 1964, Dev turned up at school with another LP record under his arm; the Rolling Stones' first album. It was to prove a landmark record for me. On the cover the first thing you noticed was that they had longer hair than the Beatles, hair being such a controversial issue at the time. They looked ugly yet, together, they looked great. They were charismatic and not being a pretty-boy I could imagine I might even get to look a bit like that if I ever got a chance to grow my hair.

The Rhythm and Blues music they had made it their mission to bring to the world was wild, rebellious, dangerous and dirty. Where the Beatles had offered to hold your hand, these guys were a real threat to the Establishment. The Daily Mirror had a headline, "Would you let your daughter marry a Rolling Stone?" Des O'Hara's dad was, like most dads, incensed by the Stones long hair. "Bunch of poufs" he called them. Men had always had long hair and it was only with the introduction of conscription in the first world war that hair was cut short. This was for health reasons to prevent the spread of lice in the trenches. Our dads had known nothing else and naturally associated long hair with effeminacy. Des had talked his dad round, explaining that the Stones were exceptionally talented musicians. Rather reluctantly, dad sat down with Des to watch Ready Steady Go which that week, the Stones happened to be hosting. As soon as Brian Jones began to speak, Des's dad was out of there. The Rolling Stone had a lisp.

I read their interviews in the music papers, where they talked of their influences and musical heroes. They enthused about Muddy Waters and had named their band after one of his songs. They introduced us to Chuck Berry, Bo Diddley, Howlin' Wolf, Jimmy Reed. Robert Johnson, John Lee Hooker, Slim Harpo, the list goes on and on. I saved my pocket money and bought a compilation blues album with some of these great names on it. Then I attended my first blues gig, seeing Brownie McGee and Sonny Terry when they played Leeds University. Ry Cooder said that discovering the blues was like getting on a train with all these great characters and I for one never wanted to get off.

I saw the Stones twice in the early days, at Bradford Gaumont. The first time there was a fairly civilised, arty beatnik audience.

Keith was playing his Les Paul and Brian his Gretsch Anniversary. Bill played his Framus bass holding it upright. I remember they played It's All Over Now with Brian Jones strumming his Vox Teardrop guitar.

The second time I saw them, my friends and I arrived early to be at the front of the queue, and managed to get front row tickets. The Spencer Davis Group was on just before the Stones and we were looking forward to hearing Steve Winwood sing those beautiful slow ballads, like Every Little Bit Hurts. They could hardly be heard for girls screaming, "We want the Stones." When the Stones arrived, the girls were trying to climb over us to get to the stage.

Brian Jones was standing right in front of me and I studied his fingers as he played guitar on The Last Time. They played a lot of their latest album, Out of Our Heads. It was the start of the soul boom and Brian played a Vox Continental organ on some of the songs. They had curly guitar leads which we'd never seen before and Keith used a fuzz-box when he played Satisfaction, something else that was new to us.

I'm just going to fast forward here to the early nineteen seventies for a moment. With no disrespect to those early rock and rollers, the greatest rock and roll record ever made was recorded by this band, under far from ideal recording conditions, in a hot dank cellar in France. Exile on Main Street is for me, the pinnacle as far as rock and roll goes. You're free to disagree of course but, in my opinion, nothing can top that double album.

I'm sorry I never saw the Beatles play live. At school it was considered rather sissy to attend a Beatles concert, only the girls and a few soft boys went to see them.

When I met Marilyn Butcher in the school corridor the morning after a Beatles' concert, I made her go over the entire evening from start to finish. I got her to tell me the running order of the songs and what each Beatle said to introduce them. She even explained in detail the shade of brown of each of the Beatles' hair.

I wasn't bothered, of course, I was a boy and, anyway, we were Stones fans.

17

The Squeezy Thing

Listening to the Stones prompted me to buy a harmonica. They were ten shillings and sixpence in those days. You have to persist with trying to bend a note until eventually, with dedication it will happen. It seems like a miracle when you finally curve down to that blues note. Next you have to learn to play "cross harp", which means, for instance, playing a "C" harp when the band are playing in the key of "G". You can Google it these days but we didn't have that luxury. We had to find out these things by asking experienced harp players.

I was trying to learn Brian Jones' playing on Not Fade Away and later, the harp solo on 2021 South Michigan Avenue, the track the Stones named after the address of Chess Records in Chicago, where they recorded some of their best work.

Eventually I discovered Sonny Terry, Little Walter and the second Sonny Boy Williamson, real name Rice Miller, possibly the greatest blues harp player. When Bob Dylan came along, I bought a harmonica bridle and discovered a different technique altogether.

Years later, I was playing a gig when I was approached by an American G.I. He produced a harmonica from his pocket. He said, "If you could do this, it would improve your harp playing," and he demonstrated the technique.

It was as if he'd tightened some muscles in his neck and squeezed the note, until it produced a tremolo effect. In The Last Waltz, The Band's final concert, there's a shot of Paul Butterfield in the last bars of Mystery Train. The Band stops and Paul Butterfield squeezes the note twice to perfection. It's totally thrilling before The Band brings it in to land on the final chord.

I went home and practiced, playing the Butterfield clip over and over again but to no avail. Maybe you have to develop those muscles in your neck when you're young but after trying until I was blue in the face, I had to confess to the G.I. that I couldn't master the technique. So, there are guys like me who just play a bit of harp occasionally and then there are proper harp players who can do the squeezy thing.

18

Mr Tambourine Man

I was sitting on the top stair leading to my attic room, the walls completely covered in a collage of posters, pictures of my musical heroes, adverts, articles and art ripped from magazines. I was wearing a harmonica bridle and strumming my guitar doing my very best Bob Dylan impersonation. "She's got eeeverythiiin' she neeeds, she's an artist, she doon't look baack."[1] My mother called up the stairs, "Sing in your own voice. You'll ruin your voice singing like that." She was right of course. Eventually, with persistence, after years of smoking and drinking whisky, I did manage to ruin my voice, but in a good way, until I finally got it just the way I wanted it.

As a teenager I learned to imitate most of my heroes; Lennon's nasal twang, Jagger's deep southern Cockney, McGuinn's California wistfulness, Eric Burden's tough Geordie. But I couldn't find my own voice in all of that, not for some years. The trick is, not to try too hard but try to sing the way you talk. Anyway, more of that later.

I first saw Dylan on TV. He was singing Gates of Eden. He was wearing a black leather jacket, wearing a harmonica bridle and playing an acoustic guitar. I thought he must be about the coolest thing since James Dean. I'd heard of him before but I hadn't paid much attention until he went electric. It was Subterranean Homesick Blues that just knocked everything out of the ball park. I bought the single and flipped it over, and there it was; She Belongs to Me. Just those two songs and I knew I just wanted to be him. Eventually I went back and listened to his early acoustic albums. It struck me that Dylan was on a level with Picasso. This guy was more than a pop star, this was high art in every sense of the word.

Dylan did awaken a social conscience in many of my generation and through his early songs imparted a certain political awareness. Would many of us have wound up in Grosvenor Square, protesting about the Vietnam war, if it hadn't been for Dylan?

19

Timber

I spent the summer holidays working at Fowler's wood yard. I'd just left school and in September '65 would be going to Harrogate Art School. Dev had left school the previous summer and had a full-time job at Fowler's. The flat-bed trucks arrived from the ports of Hull and Liverpool, loaded with timber. These were then unloaded by hand. We carried them on our shoulders and, being a skinny kid, tall and lanky at seventeen, my shoulders would get sore as I staggered under the weight.

The foreman, John Ramsey could see me struggling and would yell, "Chris, you want to stop pumpin' and get some gravy on y'taties," (that's Yorkshire for potatoes). He made a point of shouting it each day and would be in fits of laughter at my acute embarrassment every time. I dreaded the moment.

One day he didn't say it. It was almost five o'clock and I thought I was about to get away with it. As I reached the end of the yard, he watched me go through the big gate, then close it behind me. He was deliberately standing right at the far end of the yard as he watched me breathe a sigh of relief and set off for home. Then, in a very loud voice so that every one of the neighbours could hear, he bellowed, "Hey Chris.............."

When I emerged from the church after my organ practice (no more organ jokes please) I'd stand in the churchyard and listen to a group rehearsing up on Mount Pisgah, a street just above the church. I remember thinking they were pretty good. Then one day they came to my house to find me. "We're the Liberty Takers and we're looking for an organist. We've borrowed a Vox Continental for you if you're interested." So, I was in a band.

At the wood yard I'd worked five days a week, eight hours a day. I earned half a crown an hour, that's a pound a day, five pounds a week for the hardest job I ever did. The first gig with the Liberty Takers was at the Brudenell Social Club in Leeds and that night I earned a fiver.

I reckoned this was a better job.

20

Art School
(And Moses Led Me
to the Promised Land)

I was wearing chisel-toed shoes, drain-pipe trousers and a donkey jacket. It was the September of '65. I walked in the front entrance on Victoria Avenue in Harrogate and up several stone steps. Standing there was a guy who looked like the Fonz; black jacket, white t-shirt, blue jeans and greased back black hair. He took one look at me and said, "From t'country are yer? Come wi' me." He turned out to be Frank Moses and I am for ever grateful to him for sizing up the situation so succinctly and in those few words, making me feel welcome.

I was hoping to apply for the Pre-Diploma course but that required five GCEs and I'd only passed three. Coincidentally John Lennon had once had the same problem. He said, "I didn't have enough GCEs, so they put me on Graphics with all those neat fuckers." I was put on Graphics and I certainly wasn't one of those neat fuckers.

Luckily the two-year course was run by Doug Wales and Ron Swift and it was inspirational. Years later Ron said we were his best student year. I felt very blessed to be there, particularly that first year and it was a happy time for me. There was a lot of talent and some real characters. Some of them had known each other since infant's school. They'd all attended Secondary Modern Schools, like me. Paul Fielder and Mike Ingham had gone to Wheatlands, while Clive Armitage, Paul Humberstone and Bert Spragg were at Starbeck. In their final year at Starbeck, their art teacher presented them with the entrance forms for Art School and instructed them to fill them in, so it was a done deal. Now I was the new boy but it was good to feel accepted and I was soon part of the gang.

On my first day Paul Humberstone walked over to my desk and held up a cartoon he'd drawn. It was entitled Evolution. It was of a monkey who evolved into a man who then evolved into an elephant. I soon realised that

Paul was the central character in this bunch, because he possessed that rare gift of inspiring great affection. All together, these guys had an infectious sense of humour and I was more than happy to be included in their world and their endless private jokes.

Each week we were set a project. One week it was to design a poster for an exhibition. The theme was Play on Words. I was doodling on a piece of paper when Doug Wales approached my desk. I admitted I hadn't thought of a good enough idea yet.

Here's an example of how a good teacher can say something so simple and it can blow your mind. He pointed at the subconscious doodles and said "Why not use that?" Then he said "Do what you're into." By which he meant, put the things that interest you, your obsessions, the things you love, your hang-ups, your problems, your humour, your neurosis, your craziness into your art.

And at that very moment, I attained enlightenment.

The art school dances were an annual event and you were likely to meet

My drawing of Harrogate Art School, Victoria Avenue, 1967

girls with green hair and people in fabulous costume. One year, the theme was Mars Violet and some joker arrived dressed as a Mars Bar. As students we had great fun decorating the place, turning the art school corridors into dark tunnels with tinsel and tree branches. There would always be the promise of romance and of "goings on" in dark corners.

In 1966/67 we were living through a renaissance. In science we had the space race, in the arts we had Pop Art. In New York, Rauschenberg, was making wild innovations in painting where anything goes; legs coming out of paintings. The avant garde were staging Happenings. Swedish designer graphics and typography was exciting and innovative. Psychedelic posters were coming over from San Francisco. To work in advertising and graphics was considered very cool and I harboured dreams of designing Blue Note record covers.

In music Dylan released two masterpieces, Highway 61 and Blonde on Blonde. Nearer home the Beatles were at their peak, first releasing Revolver and then Sergeant Pepper with Peter Blake's cover appearing in all its Summer-of-Love glory, like the cherry on the cake. For black folks in America, it was a different story with racial tensions that still to this day, seem irresolvable. With the riots in Detroit and the Vietnam war, for many Americans, 1967 was no Summer of Love.

Although I still proudly embrace much of the hippy philosophy, neither myself or any of my class-mates became terminal hippies. We were all far too self - conscious and wearing a caftan and beads would have been ridiculed mercilessly.

What we all got from Art School was an artistic sensibility, no matter what we ended up doing. Clive Armitage became a model maker for film and advertising and a landscape painter, Mike Ingham and Frank Moses worked in advertising, Paul Humberstone became a signwriter, Bert Spragg became a photographer and I became a musician. We became life-long friends and though Bruce Sanderson and Paul Fielder are no longer with us, we get together every year to hold a "Committee Meeting."

These were extraordinary times and though I didn't fully realise it then, they were golden days. I was at art school, I was in the best band in town and it was the sixties. These days I think how astonishingly lucky I was.

21

God and Son

During my final year at school, we performed the York Mystery Plays. I was to play God and my friend Steve Day was to play Jesus. (It was type casting.) Steve got special dispensation to grow his hair, of which we were all envious because he soon acquired the perfect Brian Jones haircut and, in no time, naturally attracted an adoring female fan club.

Johnny Vincent has always been something of a political lefty like me. In the crucifixion scene, he played a Roman soldier. He said that if he'd known Steven Day would eventually become a Conservative Member of Parliament, he would have driven those nails in a bit harder.

22

The Beano Album

During that final year at school and my first year at Art School, Steve and I would get together at Steve's house. I'd turn up with my guitar and Philips tape recorder. While I was recording a heavy four chord sequence, Steve would play percussion with whatever kitchen utensils he could find. (He did eventually buy a drumkit.) We would then overdub the same guitar, along with the playback onto Steve's tape recorder. We'd discovered our own primitive version of double tracking and we liked the results. It would become increasingly distorted the more we overdubbed and one week, we played it to some school friends. They couldn't believe it was us, so we were well pleased. It was my first foray into composition and recording, be it at a very basic level, but it was an interesting start.

On Saturday nights, Steve and I would take the bus into Leeds to see a band at the Polytechnic. Queuing on the steps outside the venue the previous week, we'd seen a poster for John Mayall's Bluesbreakers. Knowing nothing about the band, we decided we'd go along simply because we liked the name, Bluesbreakers. On the edge of a crowded dancehall, before the main band hit the stage, I couldn't help noticing a guy with his back to me. He was several feet away standing between two stunning young women. I said to Steve, "Look at that guy, he must be from outer space." He had perfect jeans and that haircut with the sideboards. I watched him walk onto the stage and pick up his guitar. It was a Gibson Les Paul which I recognised because I'd seen Keith Richards play one previously at a Stones concert.

The Bluesbreakers started up and suddenly the cool guy with the super-mod haircut was bending strings. Eric Clapton looked directly at me, his face set with grim determination. He hit a blues note and that's when his guitar grew angel's wings and spoke to me. It said, "Listen to this kid, it's very important." I stood there with my mouth open and stayed that way for the rest of the evening.

I didn't realise it was God.

23

The Graham Bond Organization

Chuck Berry was playing the Odeon Cinema in Leeds. On the same bill was a band that would change everything for me. Graham Bond was a fat man who played the biggest, baddest-sounding Hammond organ you ever heard, with chipped and broken keys, through a massive reverb unit. To his left stood saxman extraordinary, Dick Hextall Smith and behind him, the blow-the-doors- off, dynamite rhythm section, Jack Bruce and Ginger Baker. In one Megaton twenty-minute set, everything suddenly came together and made sense. It made short work of the hours I'd spent working out how to play Green Onions on the piano and the nights I'd walked over to Geoff's house in our feeble attempts to sound like the Big Three. It told me that the years of studying Bach's preludes and fugues finally meant something. Here was a band combining Bach with rhythm and blues, jazz and even plantation field hollers from the Lomax's recordings. Dev was with me. He said my head went completely. The Graham Bond Organisation recorded their debut album, The Sound of '65, in the studio. It was their live set and they'd honed it to perfection.

Three members of these two bands would finally combine to form Cream. Teenagers my age up and down the country had seen the Blues-breakers and Graham Bond and the impressive thing for me was that there was no hype. It was all on a grass roots level so when they formed Cream, we already knew that was right, they were the Cream.

24

The Liberty Takers

It was a good-looking young band, four guys with blonde hair and Allan Pyrah with his dark locks. I liked to think we looked a bit like the Stones in negative. Our lead singer, Alan Perman, proved something of a liability, being a pretty boy and a notorious womaniser. Having a particularly good-looking guy in your band is a double-edged sword. He will attract a lot of girls, which is fine, until hearts get broken and then the trouble starts. The two Alans, Perman and Pyrah, had all the girls and they were in like Flynn every time. Andy Myers, the drummer, did all right too but the bass player, Tony Ridealgh, (known as Radish) and myself usually headed for the bar. We were both spotty youths and having a face like a pizza doesn't inspire much confidence. We were relative innocents, whereas Perman had already left a trail of broken hearts and a child behind by the age of eighteen. (He told me he was playing a gig when his dad dragged him off stage by the scruff of the neck on hearing his son had got a girl pregnant.) These were wild days and I'm not implying Tony and I were completely blameless, certainly not.

Johnny Vincent reckoned he got more action being a roadie with the Liberty Takers than he did as lead guitarist in his own band, The Sons of Sin.

Johnny had the keys to the van and either of the two Alans might come up to him at any time during the course of the evening, hold a hand out and demand, "Keys." Johnny's job was to handover the keys, so they could take a girl into the van, do what had to be done and then return the keys to Johnny. The perk for Johnny was the opportunity to console those girls who had been used and abused by the two front men.

One of our regular gigs was the Hole in the Wall in Bradford. Five local girls had already decided which Liberty Taker they wanted. They invited us to a 'party.' Some party. We soon paired off into separate bedrooms. It was the first time I'd been in bed with a girl. You know young guys do tend to brag but I have to tell you, in truth it wasn't easy to lose my virginity and all that Protestant guilt didn't help one bit. I had to have several attempts at it before I got to grips with the temperamental hydraulics and complicated manoeuvres involved.

Friday nights we'd load up the gear, get in the Ford Thames van and set off. Andy Myers' drums were in cases strapped to the roof-rack and Andy would naturally become concerned when it rained heavily but what could we do?

Keith Smith, our reliable and trusty driver, already had the route all figured out but I had no idea where we were going. I didn't ask, I'd soon find out when we got there and it made it more of an adventure not to know. I must've thought gigs magically appeared out of the ether. I'd no idea that Allan, or possibly his parents, or someone, had spent hours on the phone to agents, booking gigs. There were several agents, mostly Jewish guys, who took their fifteen percent and kept us in regular work. On Friday and Saturday nights we usually had gigs plus occasional gigs on week nights. Those agents looked after us and started getting us better gigs, supporting some bigger bands, even supporting some of our heroes.

Mr and Mrs Pyrah lived in the kitchen of their small terraced house on Mount Pisgah. Their sitting room had been given over to their only son, as his band's rehearsal room. When we weren't gigging or rehearsing the room was piled to the ceiling with drum cases, amps and musical instruments. Returning from a gig in the early hours, Mrs Pyrah would be there in her dressing gown, warning us from the top of the stairs, "Mind my paint work." The paintwork of course bore dozens of chips and scratches from many nights of hauling Tony's Selmer Goliath bass cab through the kitchen, along the hall to the rehearsal room. "It's alright Mrs Pyrah," we'd tell her. "We're being careful," bang, scrape, "Don't worry, it's alright," crash, thump. "It's nothing, no damage done Mrs Pyrah," ding. "You go back to bed." Allen's mum and dad were so supportive of the band and we brought in the new year with them, sitting around the table in their kitchen, playing Monopoly and partying with them into the early hours.

I lent Al Perman a Tom Lehrer record with songs like The Old Dope Peddler and the sinister I Hold Your Hand in Mine. The two of us would sing these sick or risqué songs in the van on the way to gigs, to keep everyone amused.

We had a recording of a live Geno Washington album that we'd play in the van or in the dressing room to psyche ourselves up before going on stage. Before an important gig, we'd huddle together in a scrum saying we were going to go out there and kill 'em and when the energy levels were up, we'd do just that.

In our set, the song I always looked forward to playing was My Girl. [1] After the brass riff, the song modulates from the key of C up to D. Modulations can sound contrived but the change of key in My Girl seems so natural,

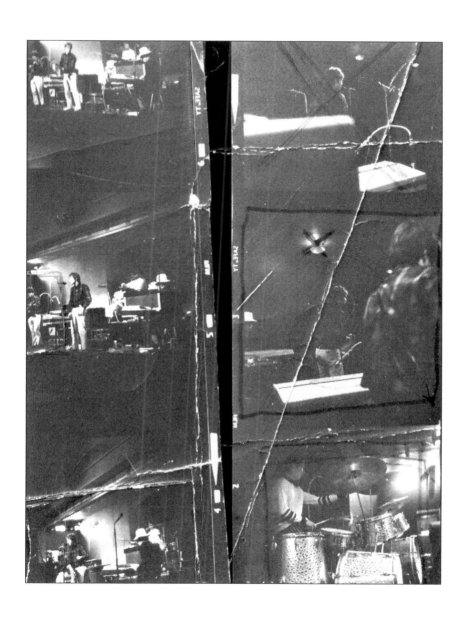

Contact prints - The Liberty Takers on stage, Hull '67
(photographed by Mike Ingham)

lifts the song and makes you feel good. To me it's an example of perfect song-writing, combined with a simply beautiful arrangement.

The Amboy Dukes had a brass section and they were everything we aspired to be. Their guitarist had a Fender Telecaster and Allan Pyrah ordered one exactly like it from the States. When it arrived in its packing case, the four of us stood there in anticipation, while Allan unpacked it and finally opened the case. We just stood there speechless. It was the most beautiful guitar I'd ever seen. It had a maple neck and you could see the grain of the wood through the translucent white finish. As the sun caught it, shafts of light filled the room, as though we'd opened the Ark of the Covenant. It was one of those moments you never forget and I've had a love affair with those Fender guitars ever since.

There's a film about Buddy Holly, which shows the Crickets playing on the edge of an ice rink and, reminiscent of Buddy, we regularly played the Bradford ice rink. It seemed very strange to me, playing soul music while people skated. Afterwards, we'd repair to the nearby Indian restaurant, the Karachi.

Some weekends, we'd play two or even three gigs on the same night, our final gig being the Blue Gardenia, known as the BG, a back street cellar club just off City Square in Leeds centre. We'd usually arrive after midnight and the place would be packed, mods mainly, including a lot of West Indians, all turned out in their finery, all dancing to the latest soul grooves. There was no chance of going through the front door and pushing our way through the crowd to get to the small stage. Like at the Cavern, there was a wooden cover over a loading bay above the stage which we had to remove. With considerable difficulty, we'd each have to drop down the hole. Then Keith Smith would unload the van and hand the gear down to us and all this while the dance-floor would be heaving. We'd eventually set up and play, then pass the equipment back up to Keith. Finally, we'd all climb back through the loading bay, leaving the joint still jumping.

Another regular gig was the Tadcaster Boulevard where they had Go Go Dancers; girls dancing in cages on either side of the stage. I found it disconcerting, to say the least, to have a half-naked girl gyrating in a cage directly to my left.

On the way to a gig in York the van broke down about half a mile from the Boulevard, so we all got out and pushed. As Keith steered us into the car park, The Steam Packet were unloading their van. We'd previously supported The Steam Packet and purely in jest, Long John Baldry had chased Tony around the dressing room, whilst he was trying to get changed. With his trousers around his ankles, Tony was trying to run away and Long John was shouting in a deep fruity voice, "That's the one I want, that little blonde one."

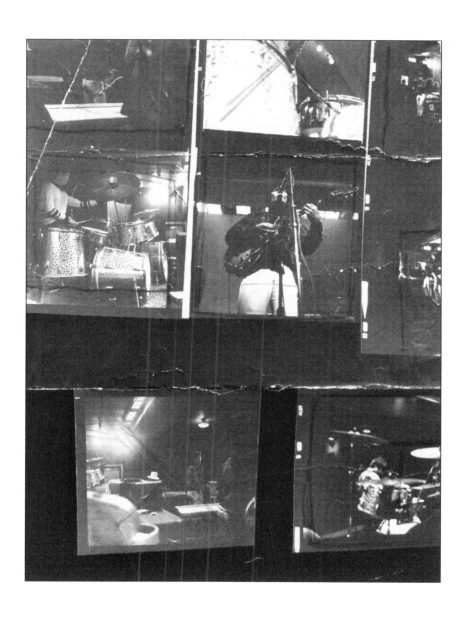

Contact prints - The Liberty Takers on stage, Hull '67
(photographed by Mike Ingham)

When we finally arrived at the Boulevard, we had a word with John and after he'd spoken to the rest of The Steam Packet, they agreed that we could use their van. We loaded our gear into their empty van, then Keith drove us to York. We unloaded their van, which Keith drove back to the Boulevard, phoned the AA, and with our van fixed, picked us up from York at midnight. Keith deserved a medal for services rendered and The Steam Packet have our thanks for saving our asses.

Despite our name, the Liberty Takers had a good reputation, regardless of the row of plastic tiger's heads we'd nicked from petrol pumps at Esso petrol stations, now displayed like scalps on the back window of our van. We were seventeen, eighteen years old. It got pretty wild at times.

You might remember the jingle from the TV ad, "The Esso sign means happy motoring, call at the Esso sign." The ad said "Put a tiger in your tank," and Muddy Waters was inspired to write a song with that very title.

In '66 The Liberty Takers played Sheffield University supporting the Fourmost. The Beatles had just released Revolver, (in my opinion, their creative peak). The Fourmost opened with Here, There and Everywhere, McCartney's beautiful melodic love song. They sang it in harmony and the five of us stood on the balcony overlooking the stage and marvelled at their rendition.

Walking along the University corridor, I spotted a notice-board. Pinned to it was a flyer for the Bonzo Dog Doo-Dah Band. I'd never heard of them but I was intrigued and amused by the photograph of this eccentric bunch, each with a cartoon bubble saying such things as, "Hi, I'm Vernon Dudley Bohay-Nowell and I play bass guitar." I took down the flyer to read it properly. This lot were well worth investigating. I stuck the flyer in my pocket. I'd learn more of them later. Packed into the lift with the Fourmost after the gig, loaded with both bands' gear and band members, we had a nervous laugh, wondering if it was going to take the weight. Would the cable suddenly snap? Luckily, we made it to the ground floor.

Some nights, when we arrived home in the early hours, Keith would go straight to work; he was a postman. You might have wondered what a fella like Keith Smith was doing driving these wild Liberty Takers around. He was a straight guy with regular clothes and short hair but for some reason, he just loved this band. I guess we took it for granted that he'd always be there to pick us up, drive us to where we were going, unload the van, carry the gear, keep an eye on us and sort out any major problems. He was a sainted man and the best road manager you could ever imagine. He would drop us off to our doors, one at a time. Al Perman in Tinshill on the outskirts of Leeds, Tony in Pool, Andy in Yeadon. Allan Pyrah, Keith and I lived in Otley. Later, when Brian Ellison joined the band, it proved a bridge too far to take him

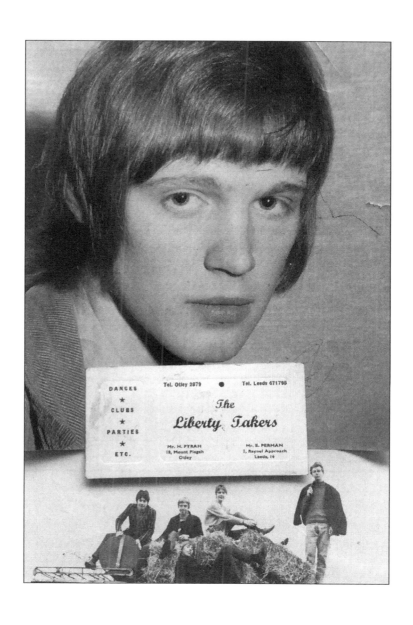

Al Perman – The Liberty Taker's lead singer with The Liberty Takers

home, so we'd leave him in Otley. Talk about dedication, Brian never complained. He would walk the seven miles up to his home on Norwood Edge. If it was school the next day, he would sleep on one of the Samuel Ledgard's double decker busses, parked opposite the bus station and arrive at school looking dishevelled, carrying his saxophone.

There were few motorways and the M62 wasn't built in those days. To drive over the Pennines, you had to navigate steep and often narrow winding roads. Many of our gigs were in places such as Colne and Nelson. I've played some toilets in my time but there was one cellar club in Nelson that took some beating, with a sewer pipe directly over the stage. It had a leak which had accumulated into a glutinous gunk that eventually dripped onto the stage, exactly where our pretty lead singer should have been standing. Al Perman stood well back from the front of the stage that night.

The club owner was obviously inured to the putrid smell, as was most of the audience, who habitually risked dangerous diseases and fire hazard in the cause of soul music.

On one occasion, our van got a flat tyre in a snow storm on top of the Pennines. We all piled out, dressed in t-shirts and lightweight Mod jackets, to change the tyre. No one had thought to bring a coat of course. As teenagers, we were fairly immune to the cold, still, we were freezing our asses off by the time we finally climbed back into the van and hit the road. When my daughters were teenagers, I recalled this incident when they'd go out wearing skimpy clothing in the middle of winter. What could I say?

Allan Pyrah told Johnny Vincent (referring to the warm engine cover between the driver and passenger seats in the van,) "In the winter, I sit on the engine, in the summer, you sit on the engine. "

One night we were playing a big theatre. The main band was the Mindbenders and I was standing by the side of the stage just as they were about to go on. Two of them were standing next to me with their guitars and matching suits. I peeped through the curtains. The place was going crazy, packed to the rafters with screaming kids. I looked back at the two Mindbenders and they both gave me a look that said, "This is what it's like on the other side kid, get used to it."

On the other side of the curtain, it was scary. You knew anything could kick off. I was glad I'd seen just the tail end of those hysteria days for myself because within a short time the screaming stopped. Times had moved on, whether it was the drugs that changed or just a culture change, who can say for sure. Suddenly everything felt different, audiences got cooler. The kids were growing up.

If you look at the Beatles' albums, they're a good indication and point of reference for how the world changed dramatically from year to year, during the sixties. Music changed, fashions changed and it was an exciting time to be a teenager. Here and in America, there was a renaissance that started, particularly after the war. Jimi Hendrix didn't just come out of nowhere. The fact that we went through all of these changes, musically, artistically, scientifically and culturally all contributed to a wealth of cutting-edge research and originality. Jazz, blues and soul music were having a heyday.

Art schools in Britain were the launch pad for much of that creativity. University and college education was free, providing student grants, not student loans, for many working-class kids like myself, who would never get those same chances today.

Many of my musical heroes went to art school, so for many musicians, it seemed like the path to follow. Unfortunately, later governments redirected funding for art education. The flowering of creativity that happened in the fifties and sixties brought a lot of money into the country, yet it frightened many in the establishment. They didn't approve of rock n' roll because the kids were finally beyond their control. As Dylan put it so eloquently, "Come mothers and fathers throughout the land and don't criticise what you can't understand. Your sons and your daughters are beyond your command." [2] When people realised they've been hoodwinked, start waking up and thinking for themselves, the first reaction of the establishment is always to shut down any trouble and call out the riot squad. There was certainly plenty to rebel against.

There is a building on Lower Briggate in Leeds opposite the Adelphi Hotel, at a fork in the road and it's shaped like a slice of cake. In the mid-sixties it was called Contact, a second-hand shop full of musical instruments. It's where Johnny Vincent and I could often be found on Saturday afternoons with our noses pressed to the windows and it's where Brian Ellison bought his first saxophone. I remember him struggling to find the notes, trying to play the riff from Midnight Hour. A couple of months later he was playing Roland Kirk solos The boy was dedicated.

The Liberty Takers bought a lot of gear from Shearer's music shop on North Street in Leeds. It was just a small shop in those days. The owner, Alex Swain, always wore a brown dust coat and there were boxes and wires, stuff piled up everywhere. This was long before they had their plush music shop in the Merrion Centre. Johnny Vincent used to try to do guitar deals with Alex; "If you knock me thirty quid off that Gibson, I'll trade you this Hofner and .....?" It was Saturday afternoon, Alex was proper fed up and he'd just about had enough of pimply kids. He didn't mince his words, "Why don't you just fuck off out of my shop." On the other hand, he could be very generous to the Liberty Takers, what with us being regular customers. If we saw say, an amp we liked, he'd let us take it home and try it, no obligation to buy. Or whenever we were short of something, he'd say, "Take it, bring it back next week." He lent us a PA system when ours broke down, and he lent me a speaker cabinet.

I eventually found an old television cabinet, with double doors. Despite my dad's aversion to the kind of music I was playing, he helped me take the TV out and replace it with a Celestion fifteen-inch speaker. I painted the cabinet white and the double doors could be opened and closed as a volume control. Neat huh.

I managed to book the Liberty Takers for the '65 Art School's Christmas dance at the Adelphi Hotel in Harrogate. Pete and Jed were technical assistants at the Art School and when they found out I was playing soul music they were keen to augment the band as they'd both recently taken up the sax. They came over to Pool Village Hall for a rehearsal and were very taken with my white speaker cabinet with the volume control doors. By the time they turned up, worse for drink, at the gig, we were half-way through the first set. Nevertheless, they put in a sterling performance, leaning against each other to keep upright while sharing a microphone. We'd never played with brass players before and this kind of soul music certainly demanded it. Rudimentary as Pete and Jed's playing was, it sparked the idea, that we should think about adding a brass section at some point, and soon.

Al Perman had a varied and continuous female following and was both experienced and inventive. I was still fairly naïve in comparison, but we were good mates and he was always a whole heap of fun. On one occasion, finding a window open, he'd climbed into a showhouse on a new estate on the outskirts of Leeds, to spend the night there with Lynne, one of his entourage.

It was a hot summer's day; me and my Harrogate Art School buddies were sitting in the small garden in front of the College when three schoolgirls, long- legged sixth formers, crossed the road, heading towards us. With their short skirts and shapely legs, these three sirens now had the undivided attention of my chums from Graphics Two. Lynne sure hadn't looked anything like a schoolgirl when she'd turned up at Liberty Taker's gigs.

Directing her mascara eyes at me, with her long dark hair looking like Sandy Shaw, with her hands on her hips, she opened her mouth to reveal a large wadge of chewing gum, and in a voice that could strip wallpaper asked, "Are you Chris from 't'Libs?" I nodded in mute astonishment and they were gone like young colts, satchels swinging down the street.

I didn't live it down. From then on, I was 'Chris from't'Libs.'

It was the nineteenth of December and at the '66 Art School dance at the Adelphi, I met the most beautiful mod girl I'd ever seen. She stood on my shoes and kissed me when I walked her outside to her taxi and she was gone. This was all brand new to me. I was in love.

The next morning, I'd find a note she'd leave for me on the notice board in the entrance to the Art School. Nothing would ever be the same.

After the dance, Al Perman and I were stranded in Harrogate and naturally he had another young woman in tow. Al had previously located an open window behind the Spiritual Healing Church opposite the Art School on Victoria Avenue. The three of us ducked down an alley and climbed onto a low flat roof, through the window and into a vestry. I slumped into a large armchair, overwhelmed and emotionally exhausted, resting my feet on a wooden plan chest and eventually fell asleep, blissfully happy. It was almost Christmas. Naively, inevitably I suppose, I would soon be destined for Heartbreak Hotel. The next morning, I learned, Liberty Taker number one had taken the current object of his affections into the church and they'd had passionate sex on the altar wrapped together in the altar cloth.

25

Oh, You Pretty Things

Istood in the wings with Skip, the drummer, and watched him stick a needle in his arm. I was eighteen, I'd never been around drugs, never even seen drugs before. When he hit the snare and kicked off the first song all hell broke loose. The sheer energy that shot delivered was frightening; broken drumsticks flying like shrapnel in every direction. "Yea Rosalyn, tell me where you' been,"[1] Phil May, hair straight down to his waste shaking his maracas at the crowd, yelling defiantly into his microphone, Dick Taylor's Chuck Berry leads exploding from his red Gibson. This was The Pretty Things in full flight and they were a force of nature.

Two years earlier, much to my dad's horror, I'd stuck The Pretty Things' picture on my attic wall. They had even longer hair than the Stones. I'm sure he must've been convinced, that his son was a massive homosexual.

Our parents had lived through a war and our generation threatened many of the values they believed in, and the kind of Britain they'd fought for. We just didn't want that world any more, we wanted a more colourful world free from that kind of religious and sexual repression. The symbol of that ever-yawning generation gap had become long hair, and sticking The Pretty Things' picture on my wall seemed a suitably poignant act of defiance.

As they finished their set, Phil May walked off stage and as he passed me standing in the wings, I noticed his lips were bleeding. I assumed this was either the result of playing his harmonica, or else he'd collided with the microphone amid the mayhem and violence of their performance. I overheard Phil tell Skip that the band couldn't afford for him to break so many drumsticks. He pointed out that they were not as popular as they had been and now the money was tight. Soul music was now the thing. Though some bands, like the Stones had naturally managed to adapt to and even set changing fashions, unfortunately, others got left behind. The Pretty Things would write the first rock concept album but the general public didn't catch on as they'd hoped. They would for ever be remembered, mainly for their pioneering early sixties rhythm and blues.

I knew that Dick Taylor, the Pretty Things' lead guitarist had been the

The Phil May drawing

original bass player and a founder member of the Rolling Stones, along with Mick and Keith. Dick Taylor, Phil May and Keith Richards had met at Sidcup art school and Dick had left the Stones to concentrate on his art studies. Phil told us if we were ever in London we could stay over at his place. It turned out that at the time, he was sharing a house with Brian Jones.

One night I was sitting with Phil and Dick and I casually mentioned that I was at art school. They told me I should think about joining a professional band when I left college as they believed I had real talent. I can't tell you how much their encouragement meant to me, coming from two of my heroes. They seemed to take a shine to me and that night Dick Taylor rolled a joint, took a few tokes and passed it to me. For a second, for some reason, I thought of my mother. She'd have been at Mrs Hannam's WI coffee morning that very day. What would my God-fearing mother think about all this? The next second, I thought what a great story it would make in forty or fifty years' time, to say I'd been turned on to drugs by the original bass player from the Rolling Stones.

We had some extra gigs so The Pretty Things lent us their PA system and said to bring it back the next week. This was very trusting and generous of them. Phil and Dick were wild men on stage but off stage they were sweet guys. Strangely, about eighteen months later I would meet two other guys whose names were May and Taylor and we would start a new band. That band would eventually change its name and sell more records than any other British band apart from the Beatles, eventually shoving the Stones into third place.

I met up with The Pretty Things again in the early nineties when we supported them at Harrogate's Royal Hall. I was in a soul band called The Blues Doctors with a four-piece brass section. I was showing Phil May a drawing of his that he'd given me back in 1966 and Dick Taylor was looking over my shoulder. He said, "He hasn't got any better." Across the road from the Royal Hall was a Cajun restaurant called the Old Bourbon, where The Blues Doctors played regularly in the adjoining venue. I had a residency playing New Orleans piano classics in the restaurant at the time. It was the place where I would meet my wife, Jane, at a later date but that's another story.

Talking to Phil before the gig, I suggested we go over the road for a drink. When we arrived, my old band-mates, Midnight Train, were setting up their equipment on stage. I'd known them since '67 and joined their band for a short time to help them out when they didn't have a keyboard player. Their bass player, Brian Duffersey, is my oldest friend from junior school. (You'll remember he lent me his Rosetti bass for my first disastrous gig with the doomed Blue Sapphires.)

Their jaws dropped when I walked in with Phil May. After the show that night, The Pretty Things, Midnight Train and The Blues Doctors wound up partying together in the restaurant at the Old Bourbon. The Pretty Things' other young guitarist got on the piano and after a few drinks, Dick Taylor produced from his pocket a collection of the very worst photographs of himself, which he passed around for everyone's amusement.

I was telling him that after I met The Pretty Things in the sixties, coincidentally, I'd met two other guys called May and Taylor and started a band. It turned out that Freddie's girlfriend, Mary Austin, and Dick's ex-wife had worked together at Biba's on Kensington High Street and were friends. This was just down the street from Kensington market where Freddie and Roger had their clothes stall. Dick told me they used to go for dinner at Freddie and Mary's.

Small world.

26

Ellison's Hogline

The Sons of Sin were all sitting on the steps of the Summercross Pub in Otley when The Liberty Taker's van pulled into the car park. The side door slid open and The Sons of Sin's singer and sax player, Brian Ellison, climbed in. Then, without a word, we drove off. Living up to our bad name, The Liberty Takers had just stolen another band's talented front man from right under their noses. I looked out of the back window of the van and watched Johnny Vincent and his band's sad faces recede into the distance.

Brian was a couple of years younger than us but wise beyond his years and ambitious. He was in the same class as Johnny Vincent and, as a schoolboy, I remember the two of them could usually be found at playtime, in the corner of the schoolyard discussing music, guitars and band gear. Brian was fifteen, so we'd sometimes pick him up from school in the group van. Doug Harrison, the deputy headmaster, would let Brian out of school early but warned him he'd never get anywhere with the saxophone, and should apply himself to his studies. He'd already been kicked out of the Grammar school for not applying himself and really didn't give a damn. Music was everything to Brian, who was determined to become a professional musician.

In the seventies, he was to be seen regularly in his platform boots on Top of the Pops. That's when he went back to visit the school. He walked into Doug Harrison's class and said, "You told me I'd never get anywhere with the saxophone. Look out of that window." Parked in the street was a brand-new Rolls Royce.

For a rock n' roll story, I reckon that's hard to beat.

Brian could network naturally and without effort. He liked people who loved music and he had a special affinity with black musicians. Eventually, years later, he would take his brass section on tour with Van Morrison.

When Brian joined the band, to make him feel at home, and because it sounded good, The Liberty Takers changed our name to Ellison's Hogline. (A hog-line is the cord around the saxophonist's neck from which the sax hangs.) One of our agents had suggested that we needed a new name because

With my brand new Selma Capri

when Brian joined, it seemed like almost overnight, by adding the sax, we really had turned into a soul band. He'd previously offered us two names; The Junco Partners and The Hogline. I'm glad we chose The Hogline, because lord knows what would have become of us if we'd had to live up to the alternative. (Junco Partners was a New Orleans classic song, made famous by Professor Longhair and Dr John, about junkies.)

Eventually we would have a full brass section. Al Perman, our lead singer, would take up the baritone sax and soon we'd have a new front man; Nelson Fletcher was a black guy who wore a suit with a matching tie and handkerchief, and who could easily have been mistaken for a young Cassius Clay. Now we looked and sounded the part, we were in business.

The drummer in my current band, John Shepard, tells me he also had a soul band in those days. His guitarist told him, "We've got to get some new threads. I've just seen the Hogline and we can't compete, they look so damned slick." We used to buy clothes at Ray Alan's mod boutique, opposite the Grand Theatre. There had also been a trip to London, to Carnaby Street where Alan Perman had purchased yellow pin-striped trousers and Allen Pyrah, pink pinstriped trousers. So, with our matching mod haircuts and new strides, we were well ahead of the game and soon attracted a discerning mod audience.

In the September of '67, I left the Hogline to go to Art College in London. Tony had left and Duffy (Brian Duffersey) joined as their new bass player. They recruited more brass players and soon had a formidable brass section. The Hogline then turned professional and backed American soul singer, Billy Stewart, on his British tour. One night, much to their surprise, Freddie King joined them on stage; he had brought along the great Howlin-'Wolf (real name Chester Arthur Burnett).

Wolf soon clocked that Duffy was the joker in the pack. After the gig they were invited to a party and Wolf and Duffy spent the entire evening sitting with a big bowl of salted peanuts telling jokes. When Brian told a good one, Wolf would spit peanuts across the room and slap Brian on the back. Duffy said, "It hurt, he had such big hands," but what a story to tell your grandchildren.

Following that, The Hogline backed Charlie and Inez Foxx on their British tour. I'd seen Charlie and Inez a couple of years earlier, when they had their big hit, Mockingbird. Their stage act was mesmerising, with Charlie dancing around Innes as they were singing. Going by The Hogline's recollections, Charlie and Inez were great performers and lovely people. Mockingbird was covered by James Taylor and Carly Simon in the seventies and they made it a big hit for a second time. Looking through my singles collection the other day, I discovered I still own both versions.

27

Battle of the Bands

Brian Ellison soon became known by his nick-name, Harvey. (I don't know, but it's likely he was named after the imaginary rabbit in the James Stewart film.) Soon after Harvey joined and before we expanded the line-up, the six of us entered a Battle of the Bands. These were always a scam; the promoter could have all the bands play for free whilst he took the door money and bar takings. The place would be packed because each band would bring its own crowd. The winning band generally received some recording time in a local studio.

The Spinning Disc in Leeds County Arcade was the venue and we reckoned we stood a fair chance. We sailed through the heats to reach the final. The big night arrived and the mods from Paul's coffee bar in Harrogate turned up to support us in their Parka jackets, with their scooters covered in multiple wing mirrors and Who stickers. Even some of my art school buddies turned up. That night the place was heaving.

We kicked off with Last Night, an instrumental featuring our new sax player, Mr Brian 'Harvey' Ellison, followed by two popular Stax covers. We'd nailed it and from the frenzied reaction of the crowd we reckoned we were winning. The Remo Four from Liverpool were a professional band, friends of the Beatles. They'd driven over to Leeds for the evening and took first prize. It wasn't really fair but it didn't matter, after all that's rock n' roll. It turned out to be one of those great nights you never forget.

When I left The Hogline in the late summer of '67, to go to London, they added Steve Isherwood on trumpet to the line-up. Steve had recently been on the Jimi Hendrix tour playing lead guitar in Leeds band, The Outer Limits and one night backstage, Steve told me he got to jam with Hendrix. I'd seen The Outer Limits when they supported The Who at the Queen's Hall in '65, and he was damned good.

Many years later, when he was playing in The C.J.Smith Band, he showed me a photograph; Jimi Hendrix is standing in the middle like Sergeant Pepper, surrounded by The Move, Pink Floyd, Amen Corner, The Nice, Eire Apparent and The Outer Limits and there's Steve Isherwood, stage right, on the very edge of the photograph.

In the nineties Harvey formed his own band, Power of Soul. They played the same soul music he'd started out playing with us in the mid-sixties because he fell right in love with it, just as he did with those early days in The Hogline.

In ninety-eight, when Jane and I were married, Harvey brought his Power of Soul to play at our wedding reception at the Sun Pavilion in the Valley Gardens in Harrogate. I wrote a song especially with Harvey in mind called Soul Days, about those times. He came to the studio and stacked up the brass parts on his tenor sax like the professional he was. We mixed the saxes so they were right up front, honking and primitive, the way they would have sounded in the sixties.

The phone would start ringing at two-thirty in the morning. Jane would say "It'll be Harvey." And sure enough, it usually was. Yet I didn't mind at all, even though I knew he'd be reminiscing for an hour, "Great days Chris, Great days." He'd have finished a gig, wherever he was in the world, had a few small sherries like you do and decided to phone one of his mates. "Do you remember.....?" I could hear him drinking, "..........glug glug glug." After half an hour he'd become increasingly incoherent until eventually I'd have to say, "Brian, I can't understand a word you're saying." He'd turned into Rowley Birkin from the Fast Show. He did like a drink but after he became

CJ with Johnny Vincent and Brian Ellison on saxophone, (early 2000's)

Alex Harvey's drinking partner, (another Harvey) he had to take some time off and dry out. Sadly he's no longer with us and he's very much missed. A lovely guy and a great friend.

28

East/West

There was a record department on the first floor of Smiths' stationers on Parliament Street in Harrogate. I was at the art school and had got to know the guy who worked behind the counter. By that time, he was familiar with my taste in American R n' B.

One day he said, "Don't ask any questions, just buy this."

It was East/ West by the Paul Butterfield Blues Band.

I played it to my mates, musicians whom I considered would appreciate this amazing record. They were totally enthusiastic and so we formed a very passionate, and yet, in retrospect, hopelessly inadequate, Paul Butterfield tribute band. I sang and played harmonica, with Johnny Vincent and Stewart Pickersgill on guitars, Duffy on bass and Andy Thornton on drums. It was the start of what would eventually become the King Bees.

We got a gig at the Stoney Lee Hotel in Ilkley and were even booked back, so we can't have been too bad. We attempted to play all the songs on the East/West album, minus the impossibly difficult title track and we might as well have called ourselves East/West. I played the Butterfield album again recently and the sheer standard of playing is still breath-taking. We were kids and I'm sure we all learned a few things from attempting the impossible, even though we were way out of our depth. At the end of the summer, I'd be going to London and who knew what surprises fate had in store.

29

The Man Who Pointed Jimi Hendrix In The Right Direction

It was Autumn during one of those pea-souper fogs in the sixties, before they introduced the clean air act. Johnny Vincent was carrying his guitar case, walking through Leeds along the Headrow, heading for his band rehearsal. As he approached the crossroads at Boar Lane, he noticed a van pull up on the opposite side of the road. A tall figure appeared, still in silhouette, wearing a wide brimmed hat. He crossed the road and his face came into focus as he emerged out of the fog. Johnny immediately recognised the familiar figure wearing a black cloak.

"You play guitar?" asked the man.

"Yea, but not with my teeth," Johnny replied.

Hendrix asked if he knew the way to the International Club in Chapeltown.

Now here's where Johnny Vincent made his first mistake. What he should have said was, "Sure man, let me take you there, I happen to be going that way myself," (Jesus, forget the band rehearsal!) On the way they might have struck up a conversation about guitars. Johnny might have ventured to suggest that, seeing as he'd conveniently brought his guitar with him, he might join The Experience on stage at some point.

Instead of which he gave the greatest guitarist in the world meticulously detailed and precise directions to Chapeltown.

To this day, when on stage with Johnny Vince, I occasionally tell this story and introduce him as "The Man who Pointed Jimi Hendrix in the Right Direction."

Following my visit to the USA, I returned to London with a new band with Johnny as the guitarist. I took him to Freddie's Kensington High Street flat and all four members of the newly formed Queen happened to be there. They were sitting around the table in the window. (You might have seen photos of them sitting at that very window.) I introduced Johnny and he stepped up to the table. Roger asked him "Do you like Jimi Hendrix?" They all leaned forward like a four-headed monster, anticipating the correct answer.

Now this is where Johnny Vincent made his second mistake.

He said, "I'm more of an Eric Clapton fan myself."

He could have had them eating out of his hand. It would have meant big Brownie points if only he'd told them, slowly unfolding the tale, of how he'd met Jimi Hendrix one Autumn night. Of how Hendrix had appeared like an apparition out of the fog in his long black cloak and asked Johnny to point him the way and how he spoke to him of many things, of butterflies and zebras and fairy tales, [1] one fateful night, down there at the crossroads.

Not long before we went to visit Freddie, back in Leeds, Johnny had bought a 1959 Gibson Les Paul, the Stradivarius of Les Pauls and now highly collectable. It was advertised in Melody Maker and the seller forgot to include his telephone number, which was fortuitous for Johnny as it wasn't snapped up immediately. Johnny wrote him a letter and arranged to drive over to Grimsby where, in January '71, he bought the guitar for £200.

At Freddie's flat, when Brian May was told about the '59 Les Paul, naturally he was keen to see it. It was stashed away in the van around the corner so Brian, Johnny, Freddie and I made our way down to the street. Standing

The Man Who Pointed Jimi Hendrix In The Right Direction

there in the street I asked Freddie what he was going to call his band. He said, "Queen." I said, "Really? Oh my god!" Johnny and Brian were now sitting on a wall, Brian with the Les Paul on his lap, amazed that he was holding this holy relic, pouring over every detail. Johnny told me he felt sorry for Brian because he knew he only had a home-made guitar.

A few months later, Johnny's and my musical tastes had changed; we were now listening to softer sounds coming out of California, which were more suited to Fender guitars. That August of '71, Johnny sold the Les Paul for £250, a huge profit, and bought a Pre CBS 1963 Telecaster.

This morning Johnny emailed to tell me that the 1959 Les Paul just sold at auction for £132,000 (plus thirty percent commission.)

At the Crossroads

30

Hearing Voices

It was that golden summer of '67, known as the summer of love. After two years at Harrogate Art School some of us were applying for other colleges. I'd applied for Bristol School of Art because my girlfriend was going there and I'd already imagined us finding a flat and living together. I wasn't on drugs, hadn't done much more than smoke the occasional joint at that time but that's when I heard the voice very clearly in my head;

"You've got to go to London."

"Why?" I asked

"Because you've got to start this band."

"How come?"

"Because it's going to be the biggest band since the Beatles, the biggest thing since the Stones."

"That's heavy," I remember thinking, finally acknowledging that the voice was real and that amazingly, it could read my mind.

"There is a down side," said the voice. "You won't be in this band for long but - and here's the up side - it will set you on a path that will be of great benefit in the long run."

"Do I have to do this?" I asked

"No, you have a choice, but you have to make up your mind right here and now. You can say no and we'll just forget the whole thing."

"That's alright for you to say, but you must know you have me totally intrigued now. What happens if I say yes?"

"You'll have to cope with them becoming world famous while you take an entirely different musical road."

"I think I understand. Ok, you' got me. I'm going to London."

If this happened to you, tell me truthfully, what would you do? Though it still seems incredibly strange to me to this day, this was the conversation with the voice in my head as it really happened. I've never heard voices before nor since and it never once got back to me.

Part Two

31

London

The Summer of Love was over. It was September '67 and we headed for London - Paul Fielder, Mike Ingham, Paul Humberstone and myself. We shared a flat in Acton, a tube ride from Ealing Art College. Some of our musical heroes had been on the Graphics and Advertising course, notably Pete Townsend, Ronnie Wood and Roger Ruskin Spear from the Bonzos. For an art school it had a good musical pedigree.

We were very much the northern contingent and we played it up for all it was worth. Being close friends and being new to the big city, we stuck together and at weekends we became keen tourists. We took in the Houses of Parliament, Buckingham Palace, the Tower, we even went up the Monument.

Photo session, Acton: Back L-R, Paul Humberstone, Paul Fielder, CJ, and front;
Mike Ingham.

Our London college friends were amused at our sightseeing escapades yet most of them had never bothered to visit those places.

We also became film buffs as there were so many films showing in the West End. We explored Carnaby Street and the music shops on Shaftsbury Avenue. Sunday mornings we would go down Portobello Road where I bought two cool Italian neck-ties from the 1940s. We went to the Roundhouse and spent the night at the Arts Lab watching a Warhol film (basically people sitting in a room, watching people sitting in a room). We visited the Tate, the National Gallery and the Portrait Gallery and, I'm glad to say, became culture vultures in no time.

Having studied photography at Harrogate, we'd been encouraged to ex-

Clive's Kitchen Rules when we moved to 42B Addison Gardens.

periment and photograph each other, which we continued to do when we moved to Acton. We'd be developing and printing these in the darkroom at Ealing. Mike Ingham had set the camera on delay and then took his place seated in front of us. The three of us were sat behind him in the dark, with just our illuminated faces creating a diamond pattern.

For a fellow student, this photograph would prove influential when it came to designing his second album cover.

It was really the Young Ones before its time, but without the extreme violence, as we rubbed along pretty well, were very supportive of each other and never had a cross word. Our old Harrogate Art School chums, who had gone to Nottingham Art School, would travel down at weekends. It was always good to see Frank, Clive or Bruce. Bert Spragg now had a job as a photographer and would arrive in London at a later date.

At Ealing Art College, Tim Staffell walked into the classroom that first day and in a Peter Sellers, silly Bluebottle voice said, "Oh. Hello everybody." Being a Goons fan, I immediately realised this guy was talking my language. Then I found out he was the singer in a band and played guitar.

Upstairs from graphics was the fashion course. Freddie Bulsara was one of only two guys on the course, and he would hang out with Tim and I. One day he picked up an acoustic guitar and sang. What an extraordinary voice. He didn't sound like anyone else. Soon Freddie would wind up on our graphics course, his musical flair a welcome addition.

32

Purple Haze

He was leaning on his drawing board staring into space, completely lost in a trance, so I waved my hand up and down in front of his face. "Where were you?" I asked him, "You were miles away." He sat back in his seat looking stunned, until eventually his eyes refocused. "You have no idea how mega I'm going to be, Chris," he said.

"How mega is that?" I asked with not a hint of sarcasm, "As mega as Hendrix?" "Oh yes," replied Freddie.

There was no shadow of a doubt. He'd clearly been staring into the future.

For Freddie Bulsara, Jimi Hendrix was more than an obsession or a massive man crush. Sitting next to him at art school day after day, I'd watch him draw Jimi Hendrix, or should I say, draw himself as Jimi Hendrix, time and time again. He'd been kicked off the fashion course probably for spending his time and his student grant going to Hendrix concerts. (Let's get our priorities right here.) How he found his way on to the graphics course at Ealing I'll never know. He naturally gravitated towards Tim Staffell and myself because our heads were crammed full of rock n' roll, like his.

I'd never met anyone else as obsessed with music as I was. Freddie loved all kinds of music so we had a lot of ground to cover, travelling from the Beatles to Bach, from Aretha to the Beach Boys. Sometimes he could be funny and camp but when it came to the music he loved, he could talk seriously and passionately for days. At the same time, he enjoyed shocking me with his sheer love of vulgarity, so delightfully outrageous you couldn't help but laugh.

From '67 till '69, Jimi Hendrix was wearing military jackets, frilly shirts and velvet trousers and no one could have ever accused him of appearing effeminate. It was only for that short period of time, that young men started dressing flamboyantly. Having lived though that time, it can be depressing looking at the relatively conservative state of men's fashion today.

I bought some red velvet trousers from Carnaby Street. I thought, wait till Freddie sees these, he'll wish he'd thought to wear something this outrageous. When I arrived at college, he was sitting with his feet up on the desk reading Melody Maker. He was wearing crimson crushed velvet trousers and a brand- new pair of snake-skin boots. He just sat there cool as can be, glanced down at my new strides, didn't have to say a thing and carried on reading.

In the days that followed we'd catch the bus over to Feltham where he lived with his parents. We were attempting to write songs but the results didn't always compare with our big ideas and fine ambitions.

Freddie would sometimes bring his guitar to college. He'd show me bits of Hendrix' songs he'd been working on, or song ideas he was starting to write. Surprisingly, for a man of his talents, he could be self-deprecating, saying, "Oh I can't get my fingers to do it, you play it," and hand me the guitar. I couldn't play it either but then sometimes, after we met Brian May, he'd say, "I wish I could play like Brian." He knew his limitations.

In his room in Feltham, he had a full- length mirror next to a huge poster of his hero. I believe he would have liked to have been able to step through that mirror and, with that left-handed guitar, become Jimi Hendrix.

And in his own way, one day, he would.

"Freddie and CJ outside Addison Gardens. (With permission Mark Hayward)"

33

Alecto Printers

I was fascinated by the print-maker and sculptor Eduardo Paolozzi. I was introduced to his work by the silk-screen tutor at Ealing when she lent me a catalogue of his recent prints. She managed to find me a placement for a week at Alecto Printers, silk-screening David Hockney's palm trees. Hockney's printer was easy going and had a laid back but very exacting method of working. When you're printing a Hockney palm tree, you certainly don't want to get it wrong.

He would carefully set up the silk screen bed, making sure the palm tree was perfectly in register with each proceeding colour. Then he would do a proof and if that was alright, do one print, check it and we'd have a cigarette break. We were smoking Old Holborn rollups with regular cups of tea supplied by the tea-boy, me. We'd then set up for the next print. It was an intense pressure and yet his leisurely attitude was very reassuring. It wasn't brain surgery, but there was certainly no room for error.

There was a ladder leaning against a wall, leading to a room on an upper level. My curiosity finally got the better of me and I asked what was up there. He said to go up and take a look. To my surprise and delight, I suddenly found myself in Eduardo Paolozzi's studio. The walls were covered in his drawings, collage material. cuttings from magazines, plans and blueprints pinned up around his drawing board. For me, it was like walking into an Aladdin's cave, with the wonderous inner workings of the artist's mind on display. Every lunch-time I would climb up and sit at Paolozzi's desk and eat my sandwiches, marvelling at my surroundings, careful not to drop any crumbs. I felt it was a rare privilege and I had that little piece of heaven, all to myself.

Years later I read that the Beatle, Stuart Sutcliff, had studied under Paolozzi when he was an art student in Hamburg.

34

Superstar

"Are you going to the church tonight?" asked Freddie, "I'll come along if you like?" I'd go to a church in Acton a couple of nights each week to practise the organ. I was rehearsing for a music exam and occasionally Freddie would ask to come along after college. He'd sit there and turn the pages for me and ask me questions about how things worked, what the various stops did, how I played the pedal board. He was fascinated by the way I crossed my hands during a Bach fugue. I guess he thought he could use that someday.

One time he pulled out all the stops and asked me to play Gimme Some Lovin'. I said, "You'll get me thrown out." He said, "Oh, go on, you play it and I'll sing it." So, there I was, playing at full volume, with Freddie singing at the top of his voice and dancing down the aisle as though he was performing at Wembley. Fat chance........

When I left Harrogate Art School and was about to set off for London, my tutor, Mike Robson, told me to go to the Tate Gallery and look at a painting by Richard Dadd called The Fairy Feller's Master Stroke. I bought the print, took it to college and Freddie was fascinated, marvelling over every detail. Eventually he used the title for one of his songs and would regularly take his friends to the Tate to look at the painting.

Freddie always liked to sit on a front seat upstairs on the bus if he could. It was the early days of Queen and the number nine bus was going along Kensington High Street; he said, "I hope the band does something because I don't want to have to work in an art studio, do you?" That was an office job as far as we were concerned. As Tim has recently pointed out, that wasn't the reason we went to Art School, we went there to become musicians.

One day at college, we were sitting at our desks, Freddie turned to me and asked, "Chris, how do you see your life? What's the future hold for you?" These were big questions. No one had ever put me on the spot before so I said I'd have to get back to him. I was quiet for a while as we continued working on our art work. Finally, my answer seemed to seal my fate, "I'd like to have a little blues-based band in which I'd be the song writer," (we were starting to write songs at the time). "I'd like to have a music room with lots of instruments. I suppose I'd have to take a job in a graphics studio.

"I'd like to have a family someday. How about you?"

Without hesitation he replied, "Oh, I'm going to be a Superstar."

35

Rebel Rebel

Every Wednesday, there was a lunchtime session in the Ealing College refectory; famous and upcoming bands would come and entertain us. There were many musicians living in the South London area, so it was an easy gig for them. Freddie, Tim and I would go to meet them and tell them we were from the Student's Union, which was a complete lie. In truth, we were there to help them carry their equipment in the hope that some jewel of musical wisdom might be imparted to us along the way. Christine Perfect did, in fact, clarify how to use pentatonic scales in major as well as minor keys, knowledge which proved valuable. She was in Chicken Shack with Stan Webb at the time, and would go on to international fame with Fleetwood Mac. So it was useful to meet these musicians. The Savoy Brown Blues Band, Tyrannosaurus Rex and Roy Harper were regulars.

We heard Bowie was playing the following week. We'd heard Space Oddity so reckoned we'd go and meet him. Tim must have been ill or something that day, so it transpired that there was just Freddie and myself, waiting in the glass- fronted college entrance, when a red tin Renault pulled up at the curb. Out stepped the future Ziggy himself, wearing blue jeans and a white T-shirt.

We walked over, introduced ourselves and told him we were from the Student's Union. Bowie opened the boot and handed us both some equipment. For some reason, it seemed important to me, to remember what each of us carried. Bowie carried his acoustic guitar in its case and a bag containing wires and microphones. Freddie carried a P.A. column and a mic stand and I carried the other P.A. column and a tape recorder.

We arrived at the refectory and Bowie looked concerned. "You guys are going to have to build me a stage." He was a man clearly accustomed to giving orders. Who were we to argue? Those big refectory tables were heavy and difficult to lift. They had a narrow lip and the only way to lift them was with the tips of our fingers, which became painful after we'd carried enough of them to build a fair-sized stage.

These days it seems almost unbelievable that myself and the future Freddie Mercury built a stage for David Bowie out of refectory tables.

The next day, we were both complaining; "How's your fingers?"

"Oh, I'll never play the guitar again."

Bowie was good though, he sat cross-legged, switched on the backing track on his tape recorder and sang Space Oddity. He stood on tiptoe on the edge of the refectory tables and performed a mime. If he'd flown around the room, you wouldn't have been too surprised. He'd already been to space after all.

I've always wondered whether, years later, when Freddie worked with Bowie, he ever mentioned that first meeting.

36

Blackbird

I was sitting in the graphics studio at Ealing with Tim Staffell and Nigel Foster attempting to sing harmonies, and doing pretty good too. Freddie suddenly picked up an acoustic guitar and sang the chorus of Wild Tiger Woman by The Move. I remember standing up, I was so amazed at the power and quality of his voice.

The Beatles' White Album had recently been released and one morning he sat down and played McCartney's Blackbird. I asked him to play it again slowly and show me the changes. Twenty minutes later, he'd taught me the whole song and it became the basis of a finger picking technique that I use to this day. So, I've Freddie to thank for showing me that.

Sometime later, when Freddie and I got access to the music department and started on our first attempts at song writing, he would sit at the piano and play McCartney's Honey Pie.[1] It suited him and it was a song he might almost have written himself; it was so Freddie. He just loved that song; "Honey Pie, you are driving me frantic. Sail across the Atlantic, to be where you belong. Honey Pie come back to me."

One day, Freddie played two piano chords that were completely unrelated.

I suggested there was no logic to it and it went against all the rules. Freddie said, "Well, rules are meant to be broken." He was right, there are no rules in music. I was already aware that, like Macca, he had a great sense of melody. He challenged me to find two complex chords that were seemingly incompatible and then, to prove the point, added more chords to them and soon came up with a tune. I was starting to understand how he composed such tuneful melodies. He told me, "Imagine the chords are rocks in a stream and the water flowing over those rocks finds its own way - there's your melody."

Many years later, my wife, Jane, and I were on holiday in Stonetown in Zanzibar, where a local guide was taking us around, showing us the sights. He asked, "Do you want to see Freddie Mercury's house where he grew up?" I didn't realise he'd lived in Stonetown as a boy as he'd never talked about his childhood. The house had been turned into a giftshop and there were

Freddie's pictures in a glass case by the entrance. The visit would eventually inspire me to write a song called Zanzibar. It was a strange feeling walking into those rooms; walls that must have been so familiar to him, walls that if they could talk, would tell a fascinating story.

I bought some postcards.

Zanzibar

There's spices all in the air on this coral island.
There's giant turtles and banana trees and monkeys in the mangroves.
While tropical fish swim among the coral reefs in the blue down below,
With the sunlight gold upon the water as the dhows sail home

(Chorus)   All on the sunset beach and here we are
*   All on the sunset beach at Zanzibar.*

They're selling African masks and just about everything
In the curio shop just off the market square
And all along the roadside, country people selling their wares.
Hear the wailing prayers from the mosques, see the ships down in the bay,
Looking out across the rooftops of Stonetown.
In the evening They're cooking all kinds of food along the shoreline
As the sun goes sinking down,

(Chorus)   All on the sunset beach and here we are
*   All on the sunset beach at Zanzibar*

Young guys are playing football on the beach
While the waves break along the shore.
White folks drinking margaritas down at the Mercury Bar.
While the little boys from Stonetown, laughing brown,
Run and jump off the quey into the ocean.
Told me you were going to be a legend and now you are

(Chorus)   All on the sunset beach and here we are
*   All on the sunset beach at Zanzibar*

Advertising campaign for confectionary, Ealing College.
(With permission – Getty Images)

37

Bedazzled

With my three flatmates, we'd set out for the West End most weekends and head for the cinema. Being big fans of Peter Cook and Dudley Moore, we were keen to see their new film Bedazzled which also starred Eleanor Bron. After the film, we went down into the Leicester Square tube station and waited for the next tube back to Acton.

When the train arrived, some of the carriages down at the far end of the platform were relatively empty. In the carriage we boarded, there was only one person and, to our utter astonishment, it was Eleanor Bron. I went over and spoke to her, explaining that we'd just been to see Bedazzled and how much we'd enjoyed the film. I pointed out that it did seem a strange coincidence, meeting her, sitting in an empty train carriage after just seeing her on the silver screen.

She smiled and was very sweet, so we sat down. Being Beatles' fans, we knew she'd starred alongside them in Help so we were keen to know how that had gone. She told us she flew to the Bahamas with the Beatles but they weren't allowed out, except for the filming. This was because the director didn't want them getting sun-tans before they shot the earlier scenes at the winter ski resort in the Austrian Alps. Still, not bad being locked up with the Beatles in the Bahamas. It would have been many young ladies' idea of heaven.

I lived in Hampstead for a while. I'd see her on the bus to town occasionally and she'd always smile and say hello.

38

Amplifier

Freddie asked me if I wanted a ticket to go with him to see Hendrix at the Albert Hall and sadly, I had to explain that I'd just spent half my term's grant on an amplifier. Tim didn't have a bass amp when we started Smile so it made sense as we could both plug into it.

I had to say no, I couldn't afford a ticket. I was literally going hungry to buy that amp but at twenty, missing the odd meal is not such a big deal. Priorities again. So, I didn't get to see Hendrix.

I thought, well, there'll always be another time.

39

Grosvenor Square

"I went down to the demonstration, to get my fair share of abuse."[1]
(The gospel according to Mick and Keith).

It's a bit of a stretch to say that Bob Dylan singlehandedly stopped the Vietnam war, but he did awaken the social conscience of many of my generation. Like his hero, Woodie Guthrie, Dylan spoke out against injustice and corruption and by now we realised the sheer power of a good song, be it about love or politics or Beelzebub. I'd say he did more than anyone to elevate popular song into a serious art form.

By the final years of the sixties, we were becoming aware that the Vietnam war was not going well for the Americans. It had never been winnable. Their government was sending more and more young guys to get killed, wounded and/or mentally damaged and yet the war continued, just to save face. In America it was almost war in the streets. You were either for it or against it. I have Harold Wilson to thank personally that he refused to send our boys to fight with the Americans, otherwise at nineteen I'd certainly have been in the firing line.

Arriving at the Vietnam demonstration in Grosvenor Square, the first person I recognised was my ex-girlfriend, who was marching with friends from Bristol. They were carrying banners and she waved and called out as the procession moved on. Susan had written to John Lennon, inviting him to come and lecture at Bristol Art School. He wrote back and she showed me the letter he'd sent her. "Dear Susan, thanks for the invitation but I couldn't lecture a deaf mute." It was his handwriting sure enough and it was signed, "John Lennon."

I was standing with Mike Ingham in a packed crowd in front of the American Embassy, when a guy a few yards in front of us lifted up a Stars and Stripes flag, doused it in lighter fuel and set fire to it. Mike had his camera with him and unfortunately by the time he got focussed it was too late, the moment had passed. It could have been the iconic picture of a historic event and on the front page of every newspaper the next day. There's film of the flag being burned, looking down, possibly from the Embassy, and there we are, Mike and me, standing somewhere in the crowd nearby.

The police drove their horses into the crowd. Someone said one of the horses was hurt and it's no wonder. It's just wrong to use police on horseback to control an angry crowd. They chased us down a street; I saw Mick Jagger running with us on the opposite side. Later there were speeches in Hyde Park; I remember being impressed by Tariq Ali. I'm proud to have been a part of that demonstration because the American government did eventually bring the boys home and stop the war.

In the early seventies I was living in Richmond and the American in the next flat had been in Vietnam. He was about my age and I'd go with him to the pub where he had to tell me about the war, just to attempt to unburden himself. I was interested enough to know what happened but he was a mess, like Christopher Walken in the Deer Hunter. He'd seen and been ordered to do terrible things, ordered to burn villages and throw hand grenades into covered pits where women with their children and old people were hiding. The poor guy, his nerves were shot to hell and he would pour down pint after pint with both of us eventually tearful as he told me his horror stories. I just kept thinking, if it wasn't for Mr Wilson, that could have been me.

40

The Smile File

This is what happened though it's not all in the history books. Tim's band, 1984, played the '67 Christmas dance at Ealing College. As friends and fellow students, Freddie Bulsara, Paul Humberstone and myself were there at the front of the stage showing our support. To my surprise, the main band that night was the Bonzo Dog Doo Dah Band. (You may recall the flyer I took off the notice-board at Sheffield University the previous year.) They were hilarious, as were their songs, often with several visual jokes going on at the same time. They were ex-art students; Roger Ruskin Spear had previously been on our course at Ealing and, as art students, we felt a natural affinity with the Bonzos and their sense of humour.

The next Monday morning I told Tim that his band was pretty good, "But," I said, "You and that guitarist were outstandingly good." I've always been able to tell when I see real talent. Tim's singing and his performance had a confidence and an assurance that I'd never come across before. That morning, Tim told me 1984 were about to fold, the college dance was their final gig. I suggested that he and I should get together with his guitarist at the earliest opportunity and so we met at a pub on Wardour street in Soho. It was obvious that Brian and Tim were great friends. They'd started playing in bands together at Hampton Grammar School. Brian was modest and focused and I liked him immediately. He suggested that he put an advert for a drummer on the notice board at Imperial College where he was studying infra-red astronomy. Roger Taylor answered the advert and, as everybody knows, the rest is history.

We went to meet Roger for the first time. He lived in Sinclair Gardens, around the corner from where I lived on Elsham Road in West Kensington. He apologised that he didn't have his drums with him; they were still at his mother's house in Truro. His mum was keen for him to concentrate on his studies and not get distracted by any hairbrained ideas about joining a rock band. Fair enough.

We explained to Roger the sort of band we had in mind and, as Brian

"They've been going in and out of style but they're guaranteed to raise a smile."[1]

had indicated in the advert, we were looking for a Mitch Mitchel type drummer. We played him a couple of songs. Roger joined in on bongo drums and we added harmonies to Tim's lead vocals. Roger, we immediately discovered, had a great high husky tenor voice. There was much talk of music and science as both Brian and Roger were studying for science degrees.

When we left Tim said, "He sings better than me. And he's better looking". We'd not heard him play the drums yet but it didn't matter, he was definitely in the band.

Brian arranged for us to rehearse in the drum room at Imperial College, overlooking the steps of the Albert Hall and there were orchestral drums stored in the corner. I referred to it as the broom cupboard.

Roger's drumkit had mysteriously arrived from Truro. I asked Paul Humberstone to accompany me as my roadie to help with my Selmer organ. Sadly, he didn't bring his camera. Brian had arranged for a mate with a van to pick us all up. When we played together that first time, there was a sound there straight away. We each played the way we naturally played and it worked.

When you hear Queen records, basically that's the sound we made that day. The distinctive sounds for me were Tim's voice which would be a blueprint for Freddie, Brian's guitar which doesn't sound like anything else plus the strength of the harmonies. Roger's voice on top above Brian's and Tim's, made the voices blend beautifully. I tried to lay down a good groove and add the occasional solo. I'm a baritone so I'd go for a "John Lennon harmony" under Tim's lead vocal.

We were sitting around in Roger's flat and he suggested we name the band Smile. Tim and I looked at Brian, who looked thoughtful for a second and agreed he liked the name and that was that. Some bands spend weeks agonising and arguing over the band name but in this case, it was agreed in seconds.

Tim designed the Smile logo and printed silk-screened posters at college, which with buckets of paste and wallpaper brushes, he and I fly-posted all over Ealing.

The logo was soon evident all over Roger's drum-kit.

Our first gig was at Imperial College supporting the Troggs. A friend of Brian's arrived with the biggest PA amp I'd ever seen. When we first arrived, the Troggs were already onstage sound-checking. There was no one else around, just the four of us standing in front of the stage watching the soundcheck. They were trying to get the drummer to play something obviously simple. There was a lot of swearing involved and we stood there opened mouthed in disbelief. He only seemed comfortable playing both hands together.

When I heard the hilarious Troggs tapes many years later, I was reminded of that soundcheck although at the time we were appalled that we were supporting them. (To be fair, Reg did write some good songs.) We sat around a table at one end of the dressing room, they were at the other end and, I'm ashamed to say, we didn't talk to them (musical snobs that we were). We were going to show them and we had a lot to prove.

I opened with Bach's Toccata in D minor. It seemed like a good idea at the time. On cue Brian played a massive chord and the rhythm section piled in. Brian lay down a heavy rock n' roll vamp and we launched into Moby Grape's Can't Be So Bad with the harmony chorus acapella. I was surprised at the sheer power of the harmonies through the big PA.

Next, we did a heavy rock arrangement of Tim Harding's If I Were a Carpenter. Then came Step On Me and a new song of Tim's called Earth. There were two more of Brian's songs, The Real Life and Polar Bear.

Years later, In the summer of 2019, I met up with Tim and Clive Armitage at Tim's local in Richmond. We were recalling pretentious band names and Tim suggested Barclay James Harvest. It jogged my memory because we'd supported them at Imperial College and I remember they had a Mellotron. It was a keyboard that played looped tapes and the keyboard player in Barclay James Harvest had very kindly taken the back off his Mellotron, at our request, so that we could look inside. We were particularly interested because the Beatles had used one on Strawberry Fields Forever.

When we formed Smile at the beginning of '68, Brian, Tim and I were twenty. Roger would have been eighteen and the future Freddie Mercury was an ambitious young man of twenty-one. Soon he would be waiting in the wings, giving us advice. He'd had a vision and now he'd foresee a way of fulfilling that dream.

41

On Broadway

The five of us were walking down Ealing Broadway, Brian, Roger, Freddie, Tim and myself. Call it second sight if you like but I remember standing back and thinking, Freddie's not in this band and yet it seemed at that moment, he was the central character in this bunch. In fact, we were all listening to Freddie holding forth about I don't know what, something musical most likely. Like Paul Humberstone, he had that rare gift for inspiring affection and eventually he would inspire people's affection worldwide. I knew how much he wanted to join Smile and that's when I decided to talk to Brian about it.

42

The Cowboy Song

Tim and Brian's song, *Step on Me,* from the band, 1984, had left a big impression on Freddie and me. Now that we'd started Smile, Freddie was always telling me, "You're so lucky to be in this band, I wish I was in it." He'd say," You know when Brian hits that chord and the drums come in and Tim starts singing, why don't you do this?"

I'd say, "Yes, thanks, I'll try that." It occurred to me that he knew the arrangements as well as we did and he wasn't even in the band. I decided I'd have a word with Brian.

I told him, "Freddie's desperate to be in this band, he sings great, also he plays guitar and piano. What do you think?" I had the idea that two keyboards in the band would be an exciting way forward.

Brian said, "Well, Tim's the lead singer, I don't think he'll wear it."

I didn't press the point.

Inspired by Tim and Brian's song-writing, Freddie started playing me his latest song ideas. He was so enthusiastic, that if there wasn't a guitar available, he would insist, at lunch time, we go across Ealing Common to the music shop. He would ask to try one of the Fender guitars, play me his song and ask the shop assistant to kindly put it back on the wall. We rarely bought anything more than a few plectrums or the occasional guitar string and after several visits I believe they got wise to us.

Freddie suggested I help him write some songs and I was under no illusions. I realised this was his way of trying to get a foot in the door with Smile. I had keys to the music department at the college; in addition to my art college course, I was studying for a music degree in my spare time, (which eventually proved a bridge too far). There was a grand piano in the music department and after college hours, Freddie and I set to work trying to write what turned out to be The Song. Freddie already had lots of bits of songs. I saw it as my contribution to help him link these bits together. He had some good ideas and as I'd never considered song writing before, these sessions began to spark my interest.

One bit of a song which stood apart from the rest went, "Momma, just killed a man, put my gun against his head, pulled my trigger, now he's dead." [1] I named it The Cowboy Song simply for reference. We'd try these bits in various sequence, the words made no sense at all but that didn't seem to matter, after all, it was early days and we were just learning. The first session was tough as none of the jigsaw pieces seemed to fit easily. I recall Freddie sitting with his head in his hands in despair, saying, "How come Tim and Brian can write songs? Why are we so crap?"

My one contribution to what years later would become the finished song was when I tried using the piano link from the Beatles A Day in the Life, [2] (Woke up, fell out of bed.....) We discovered we could link almost any two completely different bits together and it was something of a revelation. We found we could even use the link to change the time signature, go from four in a bar into waltz time for instance, so then almost anything seemed possible. Eventually when Freddie used it later, it became, "I see a little silhouetto of a man.....".

I suppose we were trying to compose our own version of A Day in the Life, only instead of just two songs joined together, why not three or even four? Hardly anyone had done that before as far as we knew, although Happiness is a Warm Gun was indicative of that direction. We ditched the traditional style of writing, (verse, chorus, verse, chorus, bridge, verse chorus.) What the Beatles were doing seemed ground breaking and far more interesting. They'd set the bar high and this soon turned into an ambitious project which we were not yet sufficiently experienced enough to complete. We knew we were on to something but it would take time so we never really came up with a definitive version of the finished song. I suppose I was the first person to hear the very first draughts though, which were built around the Cowboy Song.

Seven years later Queen released Bohemian Rhapsody and my immediate thought was, Oh, that's great, he's finished The Song.

Brian had composed a song we'd played with Smile called The Real Life. The hook line went, "Is this the real life?"

These things don't simply come from nowhere.

43

The Who

T he first time I saw the Who was in 1965 at the Queen's Hall in Leeds. Playing there is like playing inside a tin can as the sound bounces and echoes off the walls. The Who played on despite the sound quality. It was the mod era and Townsend wore his union-jack jacket. They played their hits one after another with hardly a word spoken between songs. I was seventeen and in my final year at school.

The second time I saw them, three years later, it was a Smile band outing to Finsbury Park Astoria, later to become known as The Rainbow. Freddie came with us as did my flatmate Paul Fielder. The Who were performing their new record, Tommy, in its entirety. Personally, I prefer their singles to their attempts at opera but the concert was impressive. In the van on the way home, there was much discussion and some were critical of The Who's performance. I was quite happy and said nothing. I thought The Who were magnificent that night.

The last time was at the Marquee Club on Wardour Street in Soho in the early seventies. Clive Armitage and I were sitting on the second row and I was reminded of that first time I'd stood in the wings and watched The Pretty Things' full-on assault on their audience. Again, I thought someone was likely to get hurt when The Who started trashing their equipment. This was close up and personal and certainly a dangerous place to sit. Many drummers, if you scratch the surface, can reveal a volcano that is likely to erupt at any moment. That compulsion to hit things is well channelled and Moon's drums were soon lying broken all across the stage. When Townsend smashed his black Gibson 335, shrapnel was flying in all directions. A piece landed at my feet and I picked it up. It was the piece with the oval yellow Gibson label and I stuck it in my pocket. Later I gave it to Clive who is a massive Who fan. It's now part of a collage of rock'n'roll items in a glass fronted box frame reminiscent of Peter Blake's shop window on Clive's sitting room wall.

Clive's collage including the shattered piece from Townsend's guitar (top right)

44

In His Own Lunchtime

At Art School, we gave Freddie the nickname, Pop Star Freddie. I walked into the West Kensington early evening and found him sitting on his own staring into his drink. As I arrived, he suddenly looked quite unhappy so I got myself a pint and wandered over.

"What's the matter with you, you look really pissed off."

"Oh, I'm not going to be a pop star," said Freddie, as though it was the end of the world.

"But you've got to be a pop star," I reminded him. "You've told everybody you're going to be a pop star."

And then in a mock Tony Hancock voice I added emphatically, "You owe it to us all. You can't let us down."

"No," he said, "I'm not going to be a pop star."

Then he stood up and, very slowly, looked up and spread his arms wide.

"I'm going to be .... a LEGEND."

!

45

Almighty Jeff

In 1968 I was walking along Wardour Street in Soho when I noticed a guy in a boiler suit, hands black with oil, attempting with great difficulty, singlehandedly, to push a Porsche. He shouted for me to give him a hand. I went round the back of the car and pushed as he steered it into a vacant parking space. He then came around the back of the car to thank me and I realised he was ex-Yardbird's guitarist Jeff Beck. I asked him if he was playing anywhere locally. He pointed back up Wardour Street and told me he was playing the Marquee Club that night. I asked him what time and I told him I'd be there.

Arriving at the Marquee, the Jeff Beck Band was about to go on stage. There was ex-Steam Packet, Rod Stewart on vocals, Ronny Wood on bass, Nicky Hopkins on piano and Micky Waller on drums. Jeff was still wearing the boiler suit, his hands still black with oil. He had a solo spot where he played Greensleeves which was strangely touching, and at odds with his choice of costume.

Many years later, in the nineties, my wife's best friend from schooldays, Jane and her husband, Julian, invited us to the Wembley Arena. It was a concert to raise money for Amnesty International, a kind of Secret Policeman's Ball hosted by Eddie Izzard. Before the concert, there was a reception for supporters of Amnesty like Julian. We were standing around with glasses of wine, making polite conversation, when Jeff Beck arrived with his partner. After some deliberation I decided to go over and introduce myself.

I recalled our previous meeting on Wardour Street, and the gig afterwards, which he remembered. I mentioned I had tickets to see Hubert Sumlin the following week and he started telling me how, as a boy of fifteen, in Croydon, he'd been to see the great Howlin' Wolf, (Chester Burnett,) with Hubert Sumlin on guitar. He said they had tiny amps, played very quietly and Wolf stood about four feet from the microphone because he had that huge voice.

Then he told me how, when he was eighteen, he was in Chicago and he went to a club with a promoter who arranged for him to go on stage with Hubert Sumlin and Howlin' Wolf. He said "Someone handed me a guitar. I can't remember anything I played but we did Goin' Down Slow and Killing Floor. It all went by in a flash and next thing I know, I'm in a car and someone introduces me to Buddy Guy."

He soon got around to talking about his love of restoring and building hot-rods. I recalled an interview where he was asked what success meant to him, "A warm garage." he'd replied.

Listening to Jeff's stories I was soon off in blues heaven. I mentioned the Yardbirds. He said, "They were the start of everything for me."

He told me, before the Yardbirds, he'd formed a band called the Tridents with some mates and their arch rivals were the Yardbirds.

When there was suddenly a vacancy for the guitarist's job in the Yardbirds, he secretly went for the audition and got the job.

At this point I interjected with a piece of rock 'n' roll trivia, that must have lodged itself, incomprehensively, in some dark recess of my mind. I said, "and that suit fit you perfectly."

"I'll tell you about that suit," he said, "I hung it on a hanger in the back of the car and drove back to the house, where the Tridents were sitting outside on the steps waiting for me.

"They knew who's suit that was. It was the worst moment of my life, having to tell them I'd joined the Yardbirds."

By this time, rock' n 'roll heaven had simply gone into overdrive.

"Where do you come from?" he asked, bringing me swiftly back to reality. "Otley in Yorkshire," we replied.

"I know Otley. My manager lives in Askwith, just over the river and we've spent some time there. Do you know Eddie Izzard?"

"No, I don't know him," I answered.

"He's been to our 'ouse." replied Jeff excitedly (sounding not unlike Nigel Tufnell from Spinal Tap).

Jeff was completely enthusiastic, unpretentious and welcoming. Meeting him turned out to be the best bit of the evening for me. Before we went into the concert, he asked me to tell Hubert Sumlin, "Jeff Beck says hello."

46

Shrewd Career Move

Brian, Tim and I would meet at Roger's ground floor tenement flat on Sinclair Gardens. We'd be sitting around listening to Yes and Led Zeppelin and I'd be wondering what happened to Muddy Waters and Howlin' Wolf? Why aren't we listening to Ray Charles and Otis Redding? Robert Plant's voice got on my nerves after a while and as the Stones' lyric goes "Jimmy Page was all the rage, I never knew the reason why." [1] My sentiments exactly. Very obviously it became apparent that I wasn't of the same opinion as the other three.

The music I really love is black American music as well as the Woodie Guthrie folk tradition, tracing its roots back to Scotland and Ireland. The only British bands I love are generally followers of these traditions, for instance the Stones, the Average White Band or someone like Jon Martyn who blended folk and jazz in his own inimitable way. I really would have liked Smile to become something like the Rolling Stones if I'm perfectly honest. It became clear that Roger had no great love for blues music, which was a problem for me.

The guys Roger shared his flat with were hippies from Cornwall. Roger wasn't much of a hippie; in fact, he was a snappy dresser as a lot of drummers are. He'd had a suit made at a boutique in the World's End called Granny Takes a Trip. It was beautifully tailored, in maroon velvet with piping around the edges. He looked a million dollars. Mind you he'd have still looked a million dollars in just about anything. One day he handed me an album by The Incredible String Band called The Hangman's Beautiful Daughter, saying, "You might like this." Thanks to Roger I've been a fan of the String Band ever since.

In 1968 I became a vegetarian and remain so to this day. I was in the West Kensington telling Roger of my decision when he started giving me a hard time, saying it was pointless and went against our natural hunting instincts. I reasoned that it was time we evolved as conscious beings and stopped eating our fellow creatures but it was clear I wasn't making much impression.

I suspected my becoming a vegetarian wasn't entirely what the argument was about. Maybe he simply didn't like the idea of having an organist in the band. He'd been the last to join so he hadn't had much say in the matter.

I was aware that my Selmer organ, which had sounded good in the soul band, didn't cut it in a heavy rock band. I really needed a Hammond but they were expensive and massive, required their own van plus a driver. I couldn't drive, so out of the question on a student grant.

I'm sure this had not gone unnoticed and, together with my lack of interest in the heavy rock and progressive rock to which I was being subjected, I was fully aware that the writing was on the wall.

It was half term and I'd gone back to Yorkshire. Unbeknownst to me, Roger had invited Tim and Brian down to his mother's house in Truro for some local gigs he'd organised. On their return I saw Brian crossing Elsham Road and let him know I was not continuing with the band. This presumably saved him the embarrassment of having to tell me the same thing. Sacked is such an ugly word and I like to think of it as a shrewd career move on my part!

The voice had been right, I wouldn't be in that band for very long.

After I left Smile, we all did manage to stay friends and a few years later I was living in Richmond. Roger had moved to Kew Road and I'd see him around town. It was the early days of Queen and he'd be telling me how they were getting more symphonic. By then I had my new band, Big Black Sedan, and we were into J.J.Cale, John Prine and Captain Beefheart. It was obvious that we were on entirely different musical planets.

Sometime later, Tim left Smile for similar reasons. He told me he didn't particularly like the direction the music was taking.

When they eventually formed Queen, naturally I was still interested in what they were up to and I'd call in at Trident Studios if I knew they were recording. I could just walk in in those days and they'd make me welcome, while they were working on their second album. One time we were sitting around listening to a final mix and Freddie asked the producer, Roy Thomas Baker, what he thought. He said, "I think you lot are going to be so famous, you won't be speaking to me in a year's time."

Another time I'd called in at Trident when a Japanese fan arrived. She spent half an hour going around the studio talking to the four of them in turn, then she stood at the door, waved goodbye and left.

Brian told me she'd flown from Japan and arrived in London that morning. She'd taken a taxi to Trident, talked to the guys and was now taking a taxi straight back to the airport to fly home to Japan, job done.

I called to see Roger one day and he was in a particularly good mood. "We seem to have a hit single on our hands." The hit was Seven Seas of Rhye, so his future did indeed, look bright and very soon he'd have to wear shades. With only the teeniest-tiniest touch of envy I was glad to share the moment.

On my last day at Art School, I'd taken a photograph of Tim and Freddie sitting at their desks. Tim was holding up the Who's Tommy album cover. I also took a photograph of Freddie staring straight at the camera. None of us had any idea of how we were going to earn a living after college. I was going to Canada and hopefully I'd be travelling around the 'States and wouldn't see them for a while when it suddenly occurred to me, I'd miss them.

The photo I took of Freddie on the last day at Ealing Art College, 1969
(With permission - Getty Images)

47

Trico

"Out of college, money spent, see no future, pay no rent,
All the money's gone, nowhere to go.
Any job I got the sack, Monday morning turning back,
Yellow lorries slow, nowhere to go." [1]

I got a job at Trico, a factory on the north circular road which made windscreen wipers. Johnny the trumpeter worked there. He lived downstairs in the house where I shared a first floor flat with Mike Ingham. The house was full of interesting characters; Alan Harbinson was an Australian writer who occupied the next room. It was nothing more than a corridor with a bed, a desk, a type- writer and a sink. Alan would be typing away most of the night. He would play early Bee Gees records, which I learned to appreciate, mainly for their song- writing skills.

Across the hall lived another Alan, who worked in the shoe department of a large department store. He commissioned Mike to make a massive caterpillar out of chicken wire, covered with papier mâché for the children's shoe department so that each leg of the caterpillar could wear a kid's shoe.

On the top floor lived some hippies. The day we moved in, one of the girls knocked on our door. When I opened it, I fleetingly imagined she had dropped in to welcome us, perhaps to share a bottle of wine. She looked vacantly at me and asked, "Do you have a potato?" I gave her a potato. We never saw her again.

Johnny the trumpeter lived downstairs. He was overweight and sported a jazzman's goatee. Although he was known as Johnny the trumpeter, I never heard him play the trumpet, in fact I don't remember seeing a trumpet, although I never was brave enough to venture into his room. The smell that emanated from that room, just from standing in the hall almost defies description; a mixture of sweaty socks, semen, old dishcloths and some strange fungus. Let's just say that Johnny the trumpeter's personal hygiene was perfunctory to say the least. His cheerful persona hid a tragic sadness, the subject of which he was horrifyingly keen to discuss. It concerned his ex-wife, who was unwilling to partake in his masochistic fantasies. Happily relating these fantasies to anyone willing to listen, he would be carried away on a tidal wave of enthusiasm. Being a dog was up there in his top ten, on a leash with a collar, being made to walk to heel and sit up and beg. Apparently, he had a lady friend he visited from time to time, who was rather less squeamish about accommodating his every depravity.

The band, Osibisa, lived directly across from us on Elsham Road, and they had some wild parties that went on into the early hours. Some of the West Indian guys living in that house also worked at Trico. They would pick me up in their two-tone Ford Zephyr and we'd drive to the Fun Factory as they called it, for the night-shift.

I was assigned to a machine which made bolts. The West Indian guys worked alongside me but they were fast, setting up rhythms, going like the clappers. They'd worked there some time and to them it was African rhythm drumming. There was no way I could keep up the pace. The foreman noticed. By the third night he'd given me a different job, replacing the metal boxes of nuts or bolts and stacking the full ones in the yard. Sometimes he'd call me over and send me on an errand. One time he sent me up to the top of the building where there were men in white coats. Maybe they were doing research on new and improved windscreen wipers, I don't know. Then sometimes I'd go walk about. At the far end of the factory, they'd set up car-windscreens where women were testing the newly assembled windscreen wipers. Water was flowing down windscreens and the women would attach a wiper, it would swish back and forth, they would remove it and drop it in a box. Then they would attach another. This all happened at some speed and they would do that all day, five days a week.

Mose was a checker. His job would take him around the factory, checking that the parts produced fit his templates. He was a small wiry black fella who wore a red and black striped flat cap. Everyone was glad to see Mose and I soon found out why. His side-line was supplying marijuana to the entire night shift, should the need arise. His job as checker placed him in the perfect position to accomplish this important mission.

I decided to place a small order with Mose as he was such a gregarious and charming bloke. He told me that unfortunately his supply had been somewhat delayed. Could I meet him on a certain street in Ladbrook Grove at eleven thirty on Saturday morning? He said to give him a high five when he would pass me the merchandise and we could settle up the finances later.

It was a busy street and eventually I saw his familiar face in the crowd. Mose gave me the high five, but I forgot to catch the dope and watched it fall. So now we're both scrabbling around trying to retrieve it from the gutter. He motioned me to follow him. We came to the wall of what looked like a modern factory, with just a wrought iron fire-escape running up to a steel door. Mose pushed opened the door and I followed him in. Inside was an unexpected sight; there was a flowery sofa covered in plastic for protection, low lighting, flock wallpaper, a brightly covered deep shagpile carpet. All together a typical West Indian sitting room.

Mose sat down on the plastic-covered sofa and rolled a joint. He held out his hand to offer me a matching chair, also covered in plastic for protection. Although it was Saturday, he was still in his scruffy work clothes. The contrast was made more extreme when a gold and glass trolley appeared through the adjoining door, heaped with several varieties of cake and three cups of coffee. Pushing the trolley came the beaming, smiley face of a very ample black lady dressed in a frilly pink house coat.

Coffee and cake were dually served, followed by a large reefer and after a very pleasant hour or so I thanked them both and made my exit. Mose was expanding his business and had me lined up as a small-time dealer, but I wasn't interested. I've known guys who get a kick out of dealing but I wouldn't want to be looking over my shoulder the whole time. I couldn't really see myself as some Howard Marks character with a pony-tail and a brief-case.

48

The Road to Woodstock

Uncle Eddie wasn't really my uncle. He'd been my dad's school-friend and had emigrated to Canada as a teenager. He might as well have been going to Mars as his three best friends sadly waved Eddie goodbye at Leeds station. They never expected to see him again. In the late 50s, there was a phone-call from Eddie; he arrived, looking like President Roosevelt. Eventually he brought his family over and his daughter, Judith and I became pen pals and have been friends ever since.

When I was twenty-one, he offered to pay my fare to Canada after I finished Art College. It was the summer of sixty-nine and I knew Jimi Hendrix was playing the Woodstock Festival. Maybe this time I'd finally get to see him.

The deal was that I'd work at my uncle's warehouse, Spicer's paper manufacturers, for a few weeks to pay my fare back. With any extra money, I had it in mind to find my way to the festival. Although I hadn't mentioned that to anyone yet.

In Scarborough, a suburb of Toronto, where my uncle's family, the Almonds lived, we all sat in the spacious living room and watched the first moon landing. "One small step for man. One giant leap for mankind."

It was an emotional moment. I didn't know then, but in the days to come, I would see the ticker-tape welcome in New York City for myself, when the astronauts returned from the moon.

My uncle didn't look too pleased when I announced that I was planning to go to Woodstock, but I was twenty-one, so he couldn't really stop me.

He suggested that he and I should go to the movies as he'd read a review of a new film called Midnight Cowboy. I imagined it was going to be a western but it turned out to be a warning of what could happen to a naïve young man in New York City.

I knew Woodstock was north of New York, yet I had no idea how to get there. I really wanted to see New York so I took the train into Toronto, found the bus station and caught a Greyhound bound for Chicago. It went via Niagara Falls then Buffalo and New York.

When I was a kid, Uncle Eddie had sent me a View Master, with slides of Niagara Falls in Winter, in 3D, with the falls frozen solid so I'd always wanted to see them for myself. I stood on the edge of the falls and watched the power of the water only feet away, looking down at the long drop below, imagining going over there in a barrel.

The Greyhound bus drove through the night and finally, we watched the sun come up over the skyscrapers of New York City in the distance.

As Lowell George of Little Feat put it, "Don't the sunrise look so pretty, never such a sight, like rollin' into New York City, with the sky in the morning light, - rolling through the night." [1]

I got talking to a hippy guy sitting next to me on the bus. His name was David Murphy and I told him my story. He asked where I was staying in New York and when I said I had no plans, he kindly invited me to stay with his folks. They lived in an apartment above a bar in New Jersey. What a stroke of luck, they were a lovely Irish immigrant family. The next evening, we were sitting in their kitchen, his mum serving us iced tea, and seemingly quite comfortable with our smoking neat grass, the local home-grown. That night I slept soundly, dreaming of shafts of light shimmering through clear crystal water and swirling luminous spheres with mermaids and choirs of angels.

I have no idea what she put in that iced tea.

David and his younger brother took me to see a band at a local venue, The Electric Circus. There was a light show and afterwards we stood in the dark on the banks of the Hudson, on a hill, looking across the river to the lights of New York. We were joined by a bunch of their friends. At one point they were all staring at me as I was enthusing about the view and what a beautiful, summer evening it was. One guy said, "Just keep talking man, 'cos we love your accent."

It felt good being an Englishman in New York.

David's younger brother was a New Jersey street punk. He took me to The Ice Palace, a place I believe Springsteen mentioned later in Born to Run. "Beyond the Palace, hemi- powered drones, scream down the boulevard." [2] Maybe he was there that night, or maybe he was down the shore playing with his band, Child, soon to become Steelmill.

I'd not come across him yet but I would do.

49

New York

New York was so sweltering hot that summer you needed a cold drink every couple of blocks. I had my Olympus half-frame camera with me and, having done a fair amount of photography over the last four years at Art School, I had my eye in.

I caught the subway into the city and headed for Greenwich Village. My head was full of Bob Dylan songs and stories so I was looking to find Positively Fourth Street. Arriving in the village, I immediately saw the men playing chess in the sunshine. I passed the prison where people were standing on the pavement, shouting up to those incarcerated behind the grim iron - barred windows high above. The prisoners were shouting back, having long conversations for all the passers-by to hear. I checked the bars and cafes, the streets where Dave Van Ronk, Jack Elliot, The Lost City Ramblers, even Buddy Holly had walked. Here's where Buddy lived and recorded The Apartment Tapes on his reel-to-reel tape recorder. And here's where Susie Rotolo and Bob were photographed together, walking through the slush for Dylan's Freewheelin' album cover, only six winters before.

One day, I headed for the Museum of Modern Art where the first thing I noticed was Andy Warhol's pile of Brillo boxes. Climbing the escalator, I was stunned to see, right there facing me, Picasso's Guernica. I must have stared at that painting for a good half hour because it was so shockingly powerful. I learned later that it was only in New York for a short time so I was lucky to see it. On the steps of the museum, I met an attractive German girl and we got talking; I arranged to meet her later and we went for a walk in Central Park. There were street performers and a Happening and an opera being performed on a band-stand. Later we sat on some rocks looking across to the twinkling lights from the skyscrapers, reflected in the lake, as the sun set over Central Park.

Of course, I had to do the tourist thing and go up the Empire State Building to take in those spectacular views, out to Staten Island and the Statue of Liberty. Walking along Broadway, arriving at Times Square, I saw the news flashed up in yellow letters that the astronauts were back from the moon.

America 1969.

View from the top of the Empire State Building

Later I witnessed the historic tickertape parade, the people leaning out from office windows, the tickertape floating down like strings of snow onto the cheering crowds This was truly a hero's welcome home.

Outside the bar, back in New Jersey, David's elder brother told me how he'd deliberately slammed the trunk lid of his car down on his hand to avoid the draft. I realised I was exactly the right age to be called up and sent to Vietnam. I was glad Harold Wilson had refused to send our boys over there to fight and once more I was reminded, he probably saved my life.

David Murphy worked at a book shop in Manhattan and after work one evening, he and his brothers drove me over to Harlem and past the legendary Apollo theatre in their two-tone saloon. I was smoking Cool menthol cigarettes and having such a great time I'd forgotten the reason I'd set out from Toronto in the first place, to go to the Woodstock Festival. It simply went out of my mind.

One morning I awoke early and took a short walk down the road to the New Jersey Turnpike. There was nobody on the street except an old black woman walking towards me, presumably on her way to work. As she approached, her face suddenly split into a wide grin. "Where' you from, boy?"

The Texaco Man on the New Jersey Turnpike.

she asked. She enquired about my trip and I was telling her the story. She made my day when, just as she was walking away, she conferred something on me that meant so much; she turned back and said, "Welcome to America son." I only spoke to her for about a minute but I never will forget that old lady.

I walked along the edge of the turnpike to the Texaco gas station where there was the huge plastic figure of the Texaco man, complete with black beard and checked shirt. In my head, I was singing Chuck Berry songs to myself, "New Jersey turnpike in the wee wee hours, I was rollin' slowly cos of those drizzlin' showers." [1] Then I stood on the bridge, recalling Paul Simon's song, "Counting the cars on the New Jersey turnpike, they've all gone to look for America." [2] And now thankfully, at last, so had I.

Chess players in Greenwich Village

50

Blind Faith

The first thing you noticed were dozens of Wem column speakers, fastened to scaffolding towers on either side of the stage which was considered high tech in 1969. This was the Hyde Park Blind Faith concert.

You could easily have heard Steve Winwood's voice down in central London, high above the music, but that's primarily what I came to hear.

It was evident that Blind Faith had been influenced by the first Band album, Music from Big Pink. It transpired that album had changed Eric Clapton's thinking, soon to be leaving Cream and heavy rock behind. Thinking along pretty much the same lines, I loved the new songs and lack of pyrotechnics. Of course, some people were not so sure and as I sat cross-legged on the grass in front of the stage, there were cries for Crossroads and others were walking out in disgust.

I immediately went and bought the album.

Later that summer, in Canada, I bought tickets to see Blind Faith again at the Toronto stadium. Delanie and Bonnie opened the show with Eric Clapton and Dave Mason augmenting the band. A good time country-blues outfit with great harmonies and fine songs. Blind Faith were excellent, doing more or less the same show they'd performed in Hyde Park. Sadly, they were a short-lived band and I was probably one of a minority who saw them on two continents.

Sam the Record Man was the big record shop on Young Street in Toronto. I'd already caught the train downtown from Scarborough and bought the second Band album (the Brown Album as it became known). Years later I found out that Robbie Robertson, the Band's guitarist and main songwriter, had lived in Scarborough in his youth and he must have taken that same train many times, probably to head straight for Sam the Record Man's shop. I took that same trip into town again and bought the Delanie and Bonnie album along with the new Albert King record.

Upon my return to London, I went to see Delanie and Bonnie again at the Albert Hall. For their encore, they played a Little Richard cover. Immediately several jobsworths, in brown dust coats, rushed down the aisles and stopped the show. They told Eric Clapton that he couldn't play rock'n'roll in the Albert Hall. It was strictly against the rules. Everyone, including God fell about laughing. What did they think we'd been listening to all night, chamber-music?

51

The Headless Horseman of Sleepy Hollow

J udith and I have known each other since we were kids and she's always been like a big sister. She'd planned a camping trip for the two of us and drove us from Toronto, north to Quebec. We pitched our tent on the side of a wooded valley on a clear midsummer night, with the stars of the Milky Way slowly appearing in the night sky. Short of contemplating infinity, I'd reserve the word awesome for the sound of wolves howling across a valley as night descends, It's a wonderfully chilling and truly awesome sound.

I have a book of paintings by the Group of Seven, landscape artists who painted the wilds of Canada in all its majesty and dramatic colour. The sky is so much bigger in North America and as Judith drove through these beautiful wild landscapes, I felt a strong affinity with the Canadian wilderness, one I've imagined, since I was a boy playing cowboys and Indians.

At the end of our Canadian trip, we drove south across the American border and headed for the Catskills. As we approached the town of Woodstock, I was aware that Dylan was living nearby, as were The Band. Their Brown Album, as it became known, would soon prove life changing for me and it gave me the idea of combining different kinds of roots music. It would inspire my song writing which was soon to become a lifetime obsession.

The Band had their photograph taken with Overlook Mountain in the background. The way Woodstock nestled at the foot of Overlook Mountain reminded me of Otley Chevin, with my home town, down there in the valley below.

It was late in the day and we found a camp-site at a place called Sleepy Hollow. We pitched our tent right next to a small bridge over a stream.

In the early evening, we were sitting watching the sun setting behind the trees, when an old guy, who might well have been Rip Van Winkle himself, wandered across the field from his cabin on the edge of the wood. After introductions we started telling him about our trip, until he said, "Just one minute." Returning across the field to his cabin he reappeared with a bottle of whisky and three glasses. Sipping his whisky, he asked in a mysterious way,

"Do you know the legend of the Headless Horseman of Sleepy Hollow?" He said it like it was a warning.

He began his terrifying tale. Apparently, a headless horseman can be seen on certain nights, crossing the very bridge that we were currently camped not ten feet away from. He had been known to snatch up unwary travellers and carry them away, never to be seen or heard of again.

He told us if we got scared, we could always bunk down in his cabin over the way. We didn't take him up on his offer.

The next morning, we were up early to climb Overlook Mountain. It was another fine summer's day and after a cooked breakfast we set off. It was a steep climb with the sun shining warm through the forest canopy.

"Once I climbed up the face of a mountain and ate the wild fruits there." (In a Station - Richard Manuel.)[1]

On our return, we walked around Woodstock village, calling at the post office where I cashed some traveller's cheques and bought postcards.

And still no sign of Bob Dylan.

Greil Marcus has written endlessly about Dylan and The Band, notably in The Basement Tapes. He did much to elevate rock criticism to the level of art criticism, which is where the work of both Dylan and The Band belong. There were spirits there in Woodstock village, breathing the same air. I felt close to the source and it never left me.

Crossing into the United States from Canada had been no problem. The return journey didn't prove so easy. Judith was driving and I was asleep on the passenger side, with the brim of my hat pulled down over my eyes. Remember, this was just after the biggest peace and love festival ever, and there I was looking like I'd just nodded out from a drug overdose. Canadian customs were not impressed; I was woken up by a uniformed customs officer opening the passenger door, sticking his face up close to mine and asking me to step out of the car. In the glove compartment they found various tablets that Judith claimed, quite rightly, were for a medical condition. We wondered if we'd perhaps be there for several days while they sent them off for analysis. They had us empty everything out of the car and spread it out in the parking lot. They went through our tent and sleeping bags, cooking equipment, even searched food containers. Then they started on the car. They took the hubcaps off. They had a torch and for a moment I thought they were going to take out the side panels and tear the roof lining. Luckily, they stopped short of that and I think they almost started to believe we were innocent. Still, they left us to pack everything up and put it all back in the car, not even offering to lend a hand. I replaced the last hubcap and we breathed a sigh of relief as Judith drove away and we were back in Canada.

I was just thankful the sniffer dogs were on their day off.

On my return to the UK, some people asked me if I'd been to Woodstock and I'd say I had, which technically was true (although the festival had been 50 miles from the village at Yasgur's farm). When they asked me which bands I'd seen, I'd list the bands playing at the festival that I'd seen back in England. These included Ten Years After, Joe Cocker and the Grease Band and then later, just for good measure, I added Crosby, Stills, Nash and Young to the list. The trouble with half-truths, is that eventually you begin to believe them yourself and they take on a life of their own. So, I'm coming clean about Woodstock. To be fair, it was slightly embarrassing having to admit that I was in New York, that close, and didn't manage to get to the festival.

Now, with this book, I've been determined to tell things exactly as I remember them.

Woodstock Post Office

52

GCE's

I'd just arrived back from the States and during my absence, quite a scene had developed at the West Kensington around Smile and Freddie's new band, a Liverpool outfit called Ibex. Freddie had become their singer and somehow persuaded them to change their name to Wreckage.

Because Smile was such an academically overqualified band, Freddie's drummer, Miffer, walked straight up to me and with not so much as an introduction, asked in a broad scouse Ringo voice, "So 'ow many GCE's 'av you got?" That night, everyone came back to 42b, Addison Gardens. Our flat was heaving with friends I knew and lots of people I'd never met before, including several very pretty girls. One of them asked me, "Who are you?" I had to point out that I lived there.

I called at the Ibex/Wreckage flat one day and there was a general air of depression and doom. I asked Freddie what the problem was. He said they'd just had some gigs cancelled that they were banking on. Everyone was staring hard at the floor and nobody spoke for a long time until Miffer said in his droll Ringo voice, "I just wanna go 'ome and be a milkman."

53

Smile at The Albert Hall

News reached me that Smile, now tragically reduced to a three piece, were about to perform at The Albert Hall. The only tickets left were up in the nosebleeds so Paul H and I duly made our way there. Smile kicked off the show. On announcement, Tim ran to the microphone at the front of the stage before realising that his bass guitar lead was hardly long enough to reach and he'd pulled the jack-plug out of his amplifier. Not a good start but they were soon giving Cream a good run for their money.

In a later interview, Tim said something about me being sacked going round a roundabout on the way to the Albert Hall. If that was the case it took them a long time to reach that conclusion because I'd been gone some months by then including my recent trip to the States. Tim, bless him, said I played a pink Vox Continental in Smile. For the record it was a Selmer Capri and it was grey and surprisingly, to this day, we're still on good speaking terms.

I digress. Back at the Albert Hall, now a power trio, though falling somewhat short of their previous potential, Smile opened with the theme from Space Odyssey. I'm guessing that the orchestral drums Roger was playing, had been hauled over from the Broom cupboard. One reviewer described them as the loudest band in the universe. If they weren't, with a change of name, a new front man and an injection of twenty-five thousand pounds worth of equipment from a record company, they soon would be.

Smile was followed by Free who were superb of course.

The next band up was Spooky Tooth. They had two keyboard players like The Band and I always liked that gospel combination. I would bear that in mind for another occasion.

Joe Cocker and the Grease Band performed their brilliant Woodstock arrangement of With a Little Help from My Friends but my personal favourite of the evening were the Bonzos. Viv Stanshall, swinging his microphone around his head like Roger Daltry, was only superseded by Legs "Larry" Smith's rendition of Look at Me I'm Wonderful,[1] (Two minutes Mr Smith).

127

He slinked onto the stage in a beard and full-length sequined evening dress, blowing kisses at the audience, before singing, "I'm not a bit like you or you, I'm a super showbiz star." Shades of things to come perhaps for young man from Feltham sitting in the front stalls.

What a line-up. After the show, H and I went back-stage to congratulate our friends. When the audience had gone, we wandered out onto the empty stage and contemplated all the remarkable people who had stood there in the past. The spell was broken, when two fellas in brown dust coats carrying long brooms entered stage left and started to sweep it.

Imperial College Entertainments
Committee presents
A CONCERT IN AID OF CHARITY
The National Council for the
Unmarried Mother And Child
at the
ROYAL ALBERT HALL
on
February 27th 1969
with
JOE COCKER
SPOOKY TOOTH
THE FREE
SMILE
THE BONZO DOG BAND
compered by
JOHN PEEL
Tickets 21/-; 17/6; 15/-; 12/6;
10/6; 5/-
from Royal Albert Hall Booking
Office. Tel: 589 8212
or Imperial College Cloakroom,
Imperial College Union,
Prince Consort Rd., S. Ken., SW7.

54

An Executive Position

Our friend Clive Armitage was working on props for a film of Vivian Stanshall's masterpiece, Sir Henry at Rawlinson's End.[1] Trevor Howard would play the monstrous Sir Henry, who's "rhinoceros' tyranny" would rule the roost.

Clive was making a concentration camp for Sir Henry's estate where, presumably, poachers or frankly anyone who disagreed with the Fuhrer of Rawlinson's End, could be incarcerated. Clive also made a bulldog on wheels that cocked its leg. It had a stiff lead so that Trevor Howard could push it around and take it for walks.

Working alongside Clive was former Bonzo, Vernon Dudley Bohay-Nowell. Vernon was now a member of Bob Kerr's Whoopee Band, who played local gigs around London. My girlfriend Julie and I had presented their drummer, Sam Spoons, (another ex-member of the famed Bonzo Dog Doo-Dah Band), with a rather splendid gold-lame jacket Julie had discovered in a charity shop. Delighted with the gift, Sam appeared on stage, tearing the jacket open to reveal a fake hairy chest; a square of rug stuck on with electrical tape.

At times, different members of the Whoopee Band would hold up cartoon speech-bubbles that read such things as; "He's my favourite!" when Vernon was featured on the banjo; these were the kind of mad props he would spend his daylight hours creating. Clive tells me Vernon would arrive each morning and upon entering the studio, say the same thing without fail; looking around the room, feigning surprise and exclaiming, "Yes, this looks like the place!" He assumed an aristocratic air, with a face reminiscent of the headmaster of The Bash Street Kids in the Beano. At the end of a gig, he'd put on a mortar-board and instruct the audience, "Would the girls file out of this door and the boys file out of that door."

The first time I met Vernon, I walked into the studio wearing a Chalkstriped brown, second -hand suit that I'd bought from Oxfam. (They were the height of fashion at the time.) Vernon walked over and in his plummy accent ventured, "Ay assume, you are applaying for an executive position"?

55

CSN&Y

You don't need to know much more about Marilyn other than that she was called Marilyn and she was a stunning blonde. We were on the same course at Ealing and became friends. She would take me around antique shops and flea-markets, which proved quite an education for a young man from the sticks. Marilyn was doing her dissertation on suburban architecture, a subject I'd never even considered, and she would photograph details of semi-detached houses and Art Deco dream homes. I considered her to be the height of sophistication but any romantic ideas I might have harboured were quickly dashed when she took me along to her apartment in central London. She lived in Percy Street and there she introduced me to her boyfriend who was obviously the coolest guy on the planet.

Peter Spillsbury seemed to casually walk into cool jobs. He looked like Clint Eastwood meets Peter Fonda and consequently people would invite him along, simply to add to the aesthetic. He was studying sculpture at St Martin's and when he left college, he landed a job at the Institute of Contemporary Arts (the I.C.A.) and while he was there, was hired by Chip Monck of Woodstock fame; the man who as Master of Ceremonies announced, "Would you get off those towers." (They were his lighting towers after all and he didn't take shit from no-one.) Now he was the lighting man for the Rolling Stones and before you could say, "Oh, you lucky bastard," Peter was on the 1969 Stones tour.

After the Stones tour, he told me he would be working with Chip Monck again, doing the lighting for a new Anglo-American band who were on a European tour. He seemed to think it was one of the Byrds and one of the Hollies. I knew exactly who he meant; Crosby, Stills and Nash. I'd bought their first album and was already a huge fan, so seeing my enthusiasm, he asked me along to the Albert Hall to help out.

He introduced me to Chip Monck who narrowed his eyes, looked me up and down, pinned a badge on me that said C.S.N. and Y and handed me a claw hammer. He introduced me to a roadie called Bruce. Bruce was friendly and helpful and directed me to a large wooden crate in the entrance to the Albert Hall. My job was to prize the lid off the crate and bring the very expensive, precious guitars to the stage, where Bruce would gently and reverently remove them from their cases and place them on stands. Now I've had some tough jobs in my time but for a guitar aficionado like myself, this was a heaven-sent dream come true and it didn't take me long to remove the crate lid.

I opened the first guitar case and it was Crosby's twelve-string Gretsch. It obviously wanted me to play it, of course it did. Then I placed it back in its case and made damned sure I fastened the lid safely. Next guitar, Nash's Epiphone acoustic with the double scratch-plate, I mean how could I not just give it a little strum? It virtually jumped out of its case and asked to be played.

I took the two guitars to the stage and handed them to Bruce. (In years to come he would be immortalised in Neil Young's Tonight's the Night: "Bruce Berry was a working man, he used to load that Econoline van".[1] The second verse went, "I got the chills up and down my spine, when I picked up the telephone and heard that he died out on the mainline.") The roadies mostly seemed to be from California with bleached blonde hair and buckskin jackets. The amps were torn and beat up and had obviously seen a lot of road wear. They had Byrds or Buffalo Springfield stencilled down the sides.

The next two guitars were Stills' Gretsch White Falcon and one of his vintage Martin acoustics that I knew would be worth a lot of money even then. I just took a quick look in each case and took them through to Bruce. No more time for trying them out now, the guys were wanting to get everything set up.

The band had gone off to Harrods in Knightsbridge to buy a carpet. While they were gone, I had a quick go on Stills' Hammond. It was the one I'd heard on the Crosby, Stills and Nash album. It's such a unique sounding instrument and you can hear it fully showcased on Love the One You're With and We Are Not Helpless [2] on his brilliant first solo album.

When the band returned, they decided they wanted the carpet put down on the stage, so all the equipment had to be dismantled and then put back. I was helping a couple of roadies move the Hammond, one of them was a tall guy with long dark hair. I admired the jeans he was wearing and noticed they were beautifully patched with a piece of an old guitar strap I recognised and what looked like a bit of old carpet.

Later I was walking around on my own backstage. Most people had gone off to eat or relax before the evening concert and the place was fairly deserted. Through a dressing room door, I noticed a grand piano. I recognised that same piano from the Dylan film, Don't Look Back. I sat down and I'd been playing it for a while when I heard footsteps and behind me, a figure was standing in the doorway. I turned around and it was David Crosby. I hadn't realised it was the stars' dressing room. He walked in, followed by Stills and Nash and the tall guy with patched jeans I'd spoken to earlier. I said nervously, "Hi, how y' doin'?" and slipped into the seats in the shadows behind the grand piano. I reckoned I'd stick around and even though I knew I was probably intruding - this was an opportunity too good to miss.

Crosby was carrying his famous beaded buckskin jacket on a coat-hanger in a transparent cover. He hung it on a hook on the wall, sat down at the table in front of me and, producing the required ingredients, rolled a very professional looking joint. Stills was over to my right combing his hair and checking himself in a full-length mirror. He was wearing his southern gentleman's black frock- coat and blue jeans. Nash had retrieved his Epiphone from the stage and was standing in the corner to the left of the door strumming some chords. The tall guy with the jeans was pacing up and down at the far side of the dressing room looking as nervous as hell; everyone would be there to see them. After all, this was the Albert Hall. (I wasn't aware of Buffalo Springfield at the time although I'd heard of Stills from the Supersession album he'd done with Mike Bloomfield and Al Cooper.)

Not wanting to overstay my welcome I got out of my seat and stood in the middle of the dressing room, surrounded by four guys who were about to become the biggest band on the planet with their soon-to-be-released second album, Deja Vu. I looked around at them all, savouring the moment. I said "Have a great gig, you guys," and left.

Peter handed me a joint and then we took our seats with the crew behind the stage as Crosby, Stills and Nash walked out onto the brand-new carpet, to rapturous applause from the Albert Hall audience. They opened with Suite Judy Blue Eyes and the harmonies were breathtakingly beautiful. The first set was acoustic, followed by Crosby and Nash as a duo, Stills did a solo set that was good but went on for far too long. He sang For What It's Worth which I did know from his Buffalo Springfield days. And then the tall guy walked on stage; he sat down in the spotlight on that February night in 1970 and sang I Am a Child. My jaw dropped and then I learned his name was Neil Young. What a voice and what a song. The second half of the show was electric and with their new rhythm section they played Neil's Down By The River for what seemed like an eternity, with Crosby leaping off the ground, hair flying.

Peter's friend, Danny, knew electronics so got to join them for the rest of the tour. Later he told me, one day, in Germany, the crew were late packing up for the next show and the guys in the band were helping them, wiring plugs and packing equipment. I don't know if that would happen with bands today. The joke among the roadies was; careful with the bass cabinet. At the end of the tour, Danny said they took the back off the bass cab to reveal a cake of top-quality marijuana, which they cut into slices and distributed among the crew and various friends

After the Albert Hall gig, there were many famous faces making their way to the stars' dressing room, including Donovan and Julie Felix. I was standing with Peter and some of the crew, in the corridor outside the dressing room, when a voice directly behind me spoke, and it spoke to me. It was God. He said, "Excuse me." I moved over to let Eric Clapton pass. There were a couple of steps down to the dressing room and as he reached the top of the steps, two steps down, Crosby appeared at the dressing room door. Whatever we were smoking, I watched him transform from the hero of the hour, into a small, , gnome-like figure peering up in awe into the face of God.

Peter Spillsbury, 1973

Joni Michell was sitting in the corner of the dressing room knitting a long scarf of many colours. I'd seen her brilliant performance at the Mariposa Folk Festival on the Toronto Island the previous summer. I hadn't known who she was at the time but you could see right away she was a star. It had been a warm summer night with the moon directly over the stage and she'd mesmerised the audience that night with her songs and stories. You could see immediately she was an extraordinary songwriter and performer and the audience just loved her. I told her how much I'd enjoyed her Mariposa Festival performance and she agreed it had been a wonderful evening for her too. At the end of the night, I left Joni and Graham Nash at the stage door, signing autographs, and, pushing my way through the crowd, headed down the road, high as a kite, to the tube station.

56

Stone Free

Queen had been rehearsing for some time when they invited their friends to their first showcase gig in the lecture theatre at Imperial College.On the tube on my way to the gig with Paul Humberstone, we noticed a guy sitting opposite us reading a newspaper. We could read the headline; Jimi Hendrix was dead. Shocked, my immediate thoughts were how Freddie was going to cope with the news. How could he do a gig when his idol, his alter- ego, had just left the planet? After all, this was our friend and we were rather concerned.

We arrived late and as we walked down the corridor to the lecture theatre, they were playing Hendrix' Stone Free and I just got a lump in my throat.

I remember them doing Stone Cold Crazy - a song of Freddie's I already knew - but I was distracted by the sad news and the rest of the gig was a blur.

Freddie walked right up to me when they'd finished the performance and I started expressing my sympathies but he just glared at me. I immediately realised I shouldn't have even mentioned it as it was far too raw. He'd been holding it together because he had a job to do and I should have known better. He was right of course. That was Freddie; he could make you believe you were his best friend and then another time (and he wouldn't mind me saying this) he could be as cold as ice.

57

Back Up North

I got a job at an advertising agency in Leeds so I moved back up north. I hated the job and only lasted a few months. I dropped acid with my girlfriend, Trixie, one weekend and never went back. The end of any illusions about a high- powered career in advertising.

I'd met Trixie at Harrogate Art School when she was in the year below me. And now she lived on the Oval in Harrogate. We were together for eighteen months before I returned to London with a new band. As Joni Mitchel said, "You don't know what you've got till it's gone,"[1] and that time at the Oval was a very happy time. Trixie wasn't my first love but I was hers and in retrospect, that experience seems equally important. Whenever times were bad, I'd return to those days like an oasis in my mind and I'm eternally grateful to Trixie for her love and devotion. To my daughters, she's always been like some eccentric aunt. She now lives in the mountains in Spain and we're still friends to this day.

I got a temporary job at the Playhouse in Leeds as a stage hand, working the scenery. I must have seen the Merry Wives of Windsor fifty times. I would be lowering a tree on ropes above Falstaff's head with a guy called Neil. Most nights he was stoned and once he'd dropped acid so I had to place his hands on the ropes as it was difficult for him to focus. It's a wonder people weren't injured. One night he gave me some opium. I now understood why those Pre- Raphaelite painters were partial to that particular drug. I decided I'd better steer clear in future or I'd be in big trouble, I liked it too much.

One actor was particularly brilliant and stood out from the rest. I decided I had to get to know him. His name was Tony Robinson. He came to see my band playing a cellar club in Leeds Merrion centre and some-time later he wrote me an encouraging letter when he was living in Bristol, telling me to keep playing and writing songs.

Many years later, in the 1990s, I was playing a corporate gig in Harrogate with The Blues Doctors. We were a soul covers band with a four-piece brass section and with all those mouths to feed, we needed the money. It was one of those business occasions when people get together to talk, and we just provided music in the background. As we were setting up, walking towards me was the unmistakable figure of Baldrick in full costume and in character. In his gormless Baldrick voice he said, "Oh no, not someone I bloody know. I was hoping I wouldn't meet anyone I bloody know." Still in character, he explained that he hated doing these corporate gigs, having to play the jester and introduce some middle-management boss. I guess he needed the money too and then I mentioned how much I'd enjoyed Black Adder. Still in character as Baldrick, he answered sadly, "That was a long time ago." He did introduce the boss (an enormously fat, pompous individual) brilliantly and I watched Baldrick's performance from behind a pillar so he couldn't see me and wouldn't feel too embarrassed. I later explained to Tony that I felt I was prostituting my art too and hated these corporate do's but sometimes, needs must.

58

King Ivory

ohnny Vincent, Brian Duffersey and Andy Moss, of Ladykillers fame, had recently started a band and needed a singer. Andy had now switched from guitar to drums. I'd made some tentative attempts at song-writing on my own, being inspired by Freddie's pioneering work, and I took along a couple of original songs. These met with Andy's approval, so over the next few rehearsals he encouraged me to write more songs.

We were obsessed with the first two Taj Mahal albums and spent many hours listening to Jessie Edwin Davis's guitar playing and trying to work out how they made that sound with just guitar, bass, drums and a harmonica. It was like a code we were determined to crack.

At school I'd been in the same class as Brian - known as Duffy; he was the class clown, making everyone laugh and not suffering fools. I remember hiding John Lennon's second book, A Spaniard in the Works,[1] inside a French book Duffy and I were supposed to be sharing. "Jesus El Pifco was a foreigner and he knew it." That first line was all it took and we were left completely helpless with laughter. We were thrown out of the class by Joe Thackrey the French master and told to calm down before we were allowed back in.

We were rehearsing at a youth club in Lawnswood, on the edge of Leeds. Duffy had always been fond of giving everyone nick-names whether they liked it or not. To the youth club caretaker, he gave the name Vernon Rabbit-Hutch. An eminent Harrogate guitarist would for ever be immortalised as Banana Nose. Because of his resemblance to his guitar hero, Johnny Vincent would be known as Eric Milk. For obvious reasons he named me King Ivory but by far my favourite nickname was Formica Top Smith. Duffy is a fine bass player - he can reproduce James Jameson's bass parts perfectly - yet he struggled with my original songs. Eventually Des O'Hara, of Ladykillers fame, took over on bass.

We needed a name for the band. I suggested Johnny and the Eagles, but that didn't stick; after all who'd think a name like The Eagles would ever catch on. Andy thought we needed something with a more radical edge so

for a short time we were known as Blame the System. We eventually settled on King Ivory.

Andy Moss is a several years older than us and taught Philosophy at Leeds Polytechnic. He arranged for the four of us to go into the college one weekend and record some of my original songs. At the time, Andy was married to Claire Short, who later became a front bench Labour politician. After rehearsals we would meet Claire, then known as Clara, at the Three Horse Shoes pub in Headingley. Clara and Andy were very supportive of my song-writing efforts and I began to feel more confident about presenting my ideas to the band.

Johnny was an engineering apprentice at Crompton-Parkinson's. His foreman, Vince Whitley (sometimes described as looking somewhat like a rat

Duffy

dressed in a brown overall) obviously hated everything Johnny stood for, and the feeling was mutual. "You'll never make an engineer as long as you've got a hole in yer arse," he'd frequently remind Johnny in case he harboured any illusions. Bearing all this in mind, I suggested that the band return with me to London and Johnny and Andy were all for the idea. Des was hesitant as he had a good job and didn't want to take the risk. Andy would work in Leeds during the week and join us at weekends. So, Johnny packed in his job and with a renewed sense of adventure, off we set in his van.

Duffy's Chord Chart
· D Demented with a Deluded thirteenth
· F#♭ Argumentative with an Upended Ninth
· G♭ Thelonious with E# Pretentious over B Derivative. (This is a jazz chord)
· Sonata in C flat with C views. Up the Stairs, top bell on the right

59

Park Lodge

Mike Robson had been one of my tutors at Harrogate and he and his wife, Jo, had become good friends. They told me about Park Lodge, a game-keeper's cottage that was part of Ripley Castle estate; as it was empty, they thought it might be available to rent. It was built in 1848 and situated on the castle wall at the far side of the park, across the lake.

In those days there was no road to it, you had to walk along the edge of the fields. There was no running water, just a well with a pump in the field behind the house. There was a stable which was a small building in front of the house and pig styes around the back. The place was in a bad state of repair but when I mentioned it to my parents, they seemed keen on the idea of a weekend cottage. My dad went to see Sir Joslyn Ingleby, the owner of the castle and estate, with an offer to do the place up. This suited Sir Joslyn who proposed we pay a peppercorn rent of a pound a week. He allowed us to go anywhere we liked on the estate and so my folks and I set about clearing the place of cobwebs and bird's nests, fallen plaster and general detritus. My dad and I began white-washing the walls and even decorated the main bedroom in traditional flowered wallpaper.

There was a sale at the adjoining farm, from which we furnished the place at give-away prices. No one wanted the nineteenth century furniture; a wooden backed settee, a wash-stand with a bowl and water jug, a wind-up gramophone and a deck-chair like the ones they had on the Titanic, which I still have to this day. It was like living in the nineteenth century with no electricity. We closed the shutters in the evening and lit the fire, reading or listening to 78 gramophone records by candle light. It was a very romantic setting and, as I soon found out, luckily, young women were particularly taken with the place.

My folks loved Park Lodge and were there most weekends when I was away in London. I lived there on and off for ten years before the estate eventually sold the house. The landed gentry had lived the life of Riley in this country for many years but that ended in the seventies; when Sir Joslyn died, death duties meant that his son had to open the castle and grounds to the general public. Stately homes had to become businesses and eventually surrounding lands and properties were regularly sold off to pay for the upkeep.

Years before moving into Park Lodge, there had been a curfew in the village; the estate workers were not allowed out after a certain time of night. It was still a very feudal society and there was no pub in the village until many years later. It didn't take the locals long to realise that I was not the kind of person who was going to even attempt to toe the line.

60

Big Black Sedan

I t has to be done. It's a rite of passage; even the Beatles had to do it. You haven't really paid your dues until you've spent at least a week sleeping in a van with several other unwashed, smelly, hairy-arsed musicians. In the mornings you have to find the nearest public toilet to do your ablutions. I wouldn't recommend it for more than a week, it can become rather tedious. My good friend Derek Lawrenson used to say, "You haven't had a really good night out until you've woken up in a shop door-way having soiled yourself." In a not dissimilar way, the one compensation for sleeping in the van is that hopefully, things can only improve. We did eventually find a rather grotty flat off Kilburn High Road, barely one step up from our previous accommodation.

Big Black Sedan. L-R; CJ, Peter Spillsbury, Any Moss, Johnny Vincent

We needed a bass player and, in desperation, I phoned Peter Spillsbury who was now working at The Photographer's Gallery in central London. He said "I'm sitting at my desk staring at a Fender Jazz bass that I've purchased not an hour ago in Denmark Street. It's black with a tortoise-shell scratch plate. So, your phone call is rather timely." It seemed it was already written in the stars and that's how the coolest man in the world became our bass player. Peter wasn't living with Marilyn by this time; he'd moved to a small but tasteful apartment in Barnes with its own private entrance. It was built onto the back of a large detached house. It was a small place with a fair-sized living room, kitchen and bathroom. His bed in the living room became part of the seating area during the day. The walls were painted white and, to Johnny and I, it seemed like the ideal London bachelor pad. He had a decent stereo, a great record collection, ground coffee and good quality marijuana. Naturally before long, it became our base of operations.

Big Black Sedan on stage at the Fulham Greyhound

Andy and Peter soon bonded, as bass players and drummers tend to do. Where Andy had become something of a mentor to Johnny and I, Peter too, was an education in the way he dressed, (straight leg, black Stirling -Cooper jeans), his musical taste and general demeaner of cool sophistication. He turned us on to John Prine, Captain Beefheart and the Magic Band, JJ Cale, Rita Coolidge, the list goes on.

Peter suggested we should have a new band name. He showed me a photograph at the Photographer's Gallery. It was of a young woman with long blonde hair, looking remarkably like Marilyn, climbing out of a big black car. So, we became Big Black Sedan. Another thing we liked about Barnes was the number of attractive young women around. I'd seen Julie and taken a shine to her right away; she was a tall leggy blond who looked and talked a lot like Twiggy. She had a charming Cockney accent, a great sense of humour and rakes of class. The night I met her she was dressed formally in black and white. She looked stunning and we held our gaze for far too long but from then on, she kept her distance.

She was a wild girl. All of these women were friends and some had become very good friends. A combination of mandrax and alcohol used to fuel some wild all-female parties. It was the early seventies in London and people were keen to experiment sexually. These women were all in cahoots and I think Julie was waiting for me to have had enough fun with all the other girls. I must have been approaching double figures before she made her move. She'd been around the block a lot more than I'd ever dreamed and she was just the kind of education every young man needs. We were together about eighteen months. Friends with benefits would be a polite way to describe my time with Julie and I wouldn't have missed it for the world.

61

Temporarily Out of Action

When Queen first got a record deal, I saw Freddie in Kensington Market and he told me, "We got our equipment." I asked him how much musical equipment and he said "Twenty-five grand's worth." My jaw dropped. Sometime later, on arriving back in London I called round to see Freddie. He was living on Kensington High Street, which was some improvement on the grotty student flats we'd all grown accustomed to. He and his girlfriend, Mary Austin, had made a home with sumptuous Biba-inspired décor. Mary worked at Biba's department store just down the road and Queen's first album shots were taken in their first floor flat.

One evening, I ran into Freddie and Mary outside Biba's. They were dressed to the nines, obviously going out for the evening, there in all their finery, waiting for a number nine bus. They looked quite incongruous standing at the bus stop, with Freddie, already every inch the rock star and Mary looking simply wonderful. And what a handsome couple they made.

At their flat, Freddie had an upright piano next to their bed so that, should the maestro feel inspired during the night, he could Immediately launch into his latest work of genius. He told me Mary wasn't particularly overjoyed with the arrangement. I was keen to show him my first batch of songs. After all, those piano sessions at Ealing had sparked my interest in song writing for which I am eternally grateful. He explained that he was full of cold as I sat on the edge of the bed and played him my songs. Freddie was always a good listener and eventually, when I stopped playing, he said, "You've cracked it, Chris." It meant a lot to me, to get Freddie's approval.

He was also very competitive and, when I'd gone, I'm sure he sat down and wrote Killer Queen.[1] I can't be absolutely sure but there were a few clues. He was "temporarily out of action," and "for cars he couldn't care less,"(Big Black Sedan being the name of my new band.) Maybe I'm imagining it but there was a vibe about the songs I'd been writing that was apparent in several of his songs which appeared on the Sheer Heart Attack Album. That's ok with me, I'm not complaining, it's the way it works. He showed me the ropes and I guess he got something back in return.

62

Illustra

Bobby Harrison had been the original drummer with Procol Harum and lived in the big house adjoining Peter's flat. He put us in touch with a guy in Soho who owned an advertising film company and was looking for a band to manage. Barry Palin kindly let us use his film studio, Illustra, for our rehearsals on Sunday afternoons. It had a small projection room at the back and it was warm and comfortable. Just down the road was an Italian family bistro serving delicious pizzas and pasta and after rehearsals, we'd usually wind up there. There was even a pub a couple of doors down and surprisingly, we felt we'd landed on our feet.

(Back up north, Johnny told his pal, Andy Thornton, about the bistro. Andy replied with as much contempt as he could summon, "Beestroh? A beestroh? That's not in the Yorkshire dictionary.")

One of our first gigs was at Photographer's Gallery and as Peter still had connections with The Stones' road crew, we were able to borrow Charley Watts' spare drum riser for Andy Moss. Then Peter arranged for one of his favourite photographers from the Gallery, to come to Illustra and take pictures of the band while we were rehearsing. The lighting in the film studio was subdued and tasteful and the guy did an excellent job so we were happy with the results.

Barry lived in the penthouse flat on the top floor of the building. He was in his early thirties, drove an Aston Martin DB5 and clearly aspired to a James Bond lifestyle. For a while, he was going out with the actress Amy McDonald. Standing at the bar at Ronnie Scot's, Barry pulled out the biggest wad of notes I'd ever seen. He was a man about town and a local in Soho, knowing everyone from the working girls to the paper boy. He was a smart suited gentleman with connections and we thought we'd found our Brian Epstein.

He showed an interest in promoting Big Black Sedan and introduced us to Roger Watson, a young guy who was beginning to make a name for himself in the music business. Johnny and I recorded some rough demos in Roger's basement flat, then Barry put up the money for the band to record some of the songs at Mayfair Sound in Central London. Arriving at Mayfair, Alvin

Stardust was just winding up a recording session. He'd previously had hits in his former incarnation as early sixties teen-idol Shane Fenton. Now he'd been rebranded with his dyed black quiff, black leather gear, complete with one black leather glove. Alvin hadn't dressed down for the session, here he was in his full regalia. To be fair, perhaps he had a photo-shoot that day but I like to think he dressed like that all the time. After all, I once saw Bowie in Biba's with the wife and kids and he was dressed as Ziggy Stardust; tights, make-up, the full works, so nothing would surprise me.

At lunch-break, during the recording session, I took Peter and Andrew along the road to Trident where I knew Queen were recording that day, and introduced them. While Brian was layering guitar parts next door in the studio, Jimi Hendrix style, the others were sitting around, watching TV. Eventually Roger Taylor suggested they play us a track they'd been working on called Liar. My rhythm section was obviously less than impressed and I could see them both squirming with discomfort. Freddie started glowering at their negative response. I felt embarrassed and we beat a hasty retreat; I guess you can't win 'em all.

Peter Spillsbury with Andy Moss in the background at Illustra

Roger Watson took our Mayfair recordings to Chrysalis and somehow or other, managed to land himself a job as A&R man (Artists and Repertoire). Chrysalis showed some interest and then Steve Stephenson from Chapel's, the big music publishers, heard the songs and was very enthusiastic. So, we were off to an auspicious start. We'd been lucky so far and it seemed like all our ducks were in a row.

What could possibly go wrong?

63

The Missing Chapter

Whenever I think about the time I accidentally put my foot through Brian May's guitar, I'm determined that it's something I should keep to myself. The sheer buttock-clenching horror and embarrassment is something I'd prefer to remain hidden.

I had just discovered that a young woman, who did look a lot like Joan Jett, and incidentally happened to have been my first love, had been shagging my best friend, a lead singer. Currently, she was now shagging another friend, who, coincidentally, was also a lead singer. I won't depress you with the details; I was obviously very distracted.

Unnoticed by me, Brian's acoustic guitar was leaning at a precarious angle of approximately forty-five degrees against the back of her sofa, on which Freddie and Roger were sitting.

I'm reluctant to conjure up the picture of Brian standing there, holding the shattered guitar neck in one hand and the smashed body in the other, held together by one or two guitar strings.

That wasn't the only thing that was broken that night.

Brian was so nice, far too nice, standing there holding the remnants of his precious acoustic which had probably cost him most of his student grant. He said, "It's all right, Chris."

It really wasn't.

For all the bands I've been in and the music I've written, published and performed, it would be a dreadful irony, if I became famous for being the man who put his foot through Brian May's guitar.

64

Hard Luck Story

Now I had the ear of Steve Stephenson, a very astute young Jewish guy. He was an A&R man at Chapel Music, eventually to become Warner Chapel, the most prestigious music publishing company known to man. Steve was sending my songs to various people including Ray Charles. I received a message back from Ray, saying he liked the songs but didn't think I was there yet. He told me to keep writing and added that I had great potential. He was absolutely right, that's all I had. It would be years before I had the skill and experience to write the kind of songs, I felt I was capable of writing. That encouragement meant a lot though, words from the master.

Steve sent my songs to Allan Clarke, the lead singer with the Hollies, who was wanting to make a solo record. I assume he was frustrated with the Hollies as they seemed like yesterday's group. His best friend Graham Nash was becoming the nearest thing to the Beatles with C.S.N.&Y. At that time, Clarke was looking for one young songwriter to write an entire album for him. Word came back from his management that they liked my songs and they invited us to meet over breakfast at the Dorchester.

Steve and I arrived at the Dorchester and ordered breakfast. In the early seventies, there was an obscene amount of money around in the music business. Records were selling and music meant everything to most young people. (It was going to save the world, remember.) We ordered champagne on Warner Brothers' expense account. I'd been sleeping on Johnny Vincent's couch and living on cornflakes, so breakfast at the Dorchester was a welcome respite from near-starvation.

Steve's average day was, frankly, Epicurean. He'd arrive at his office at Marble Arch about ten and phone his wife. Then he'd make several phone-calls and arrange to meet someone for a business lunch. Lunch could go on for several hours, sometimes late into the afternoon. Then he'd return to the office, outside which several musicians might well have spent the entire afternoon waiting. He'd see them, make a couple more phone-calls, phone his wife again and take a taxi home to Bayswater. Surprisingly though, he did get results.

I once waited outside Steve's office all afternoon, while he was in there with Rick Parfitt, presumably celebrating the success of the latest Status Quo record. Nowadays, I would probably walk in there and say, "Come on, give me a drink, Steve, I'm dying of thirst out there," but I wasn't so confident in those days. The hilarity became louder and louder, as secretaries kept walking in with more bottles of champaign, until eventually they both staggered out completely blotto.

Meanwhile back at the Dorchester, we'd finished breakfast, polished off the champagne and still no sign of Allan Clarke and his manager. We arrived back at the office and the phone was ringing. It was Clarke's manager and he apologised for not showing up. "We had a promo record arrive from America and much as we love your boy's work," he told Steve, "we've decided to go with the American kid."

Steve was sitting at his desk holding the phone. I was standing next to him, leaning close to his ear so I could catch the conversation. "Tell him I want to hear this American kid," I said, "and he'd better be good."

Twenty minutes later, a motor cycle courier arrived. Inside the envelope was a vinyl album with a white label, on which was written, in biro, "Greetings from Ashbury Park/ Bruce Springsteen."

"Get it on the turn-table, Steve. This had better be brilliant." It was.

We listened to side one. I said "Turn it over," We listened to side two and before it was half way through, I started laughing. I said Steve, "I've just been aced by the best."

When I left the office, I walked down the street laughing to myself, shaking my head in disbelief. Fair enough. I was already a lifelong Bruce fan.

65

The Cape

Freddie and Roger ran a stall in Kensington Market selling platform shoes, boots, a variety of fashionable clothing and some of Freddie's college drawings of Jimi Hendrix. (In retrospect, the drawings would have been a sound investment.) That day as I approached the stall, Freddie was standing there with his arms spread, wearing a white silk pleated cape (you know the one). I didn't say a word, just walked around him and then it just came out of my mouth. "You're not actually going to wear that are you?" Freddie did a twirl around. "But it's beautiful," he insisted.

A woman with orange hair was kneeling at his feet struggling to fit the cape. "Stand still Freddie, I can't pin it when you're moving around like that." She glared at me.

"Brian's having one made as well", Freddie added.

"Oh, that'll be nice," I said not without a hint of sarcasm.

Many years later, I was sitting in a dentist's waiting room, thumbing through a magazine when I came across an article about the woman with the orange hair, and it mentioned that she had designed the capes for Freddie and Brian. It turns out I'd insulted Zandra Rhodes.

66

Perfect

I always enjoyed reading Freddie's interviews in the music press because he was in his element and he was always guaranteed to say something witty or shockingly outrageous. Lee "Scratch" Perry, the Jamaican Reggie producer said Freddie was a devil and I'm sure he was right.

My favourite Freddie interview was when a journalist commented rather rudely on the size of his teeth. You might have expected Freddie to come back with the obvious reply or demolish the journalist with some equally derogatory remark. He didn't.

"Oh yes, I keep meaning to have something done with them but I never quite get round to it," he said. Then glancing down at his body, "Apart from that, I'm perfect."

67

The 1974 Tour

Before the University tour, I explained to Chrysalis that I wasn't really a solo performer. They told me, "You are now," so I was ushered onto the stage, for the first time ever, with just an acoustic guitar and occasionally a piano if there happened to be one. It was daunting but after a couple of nights, I began to take it in my stride. I was supporting Bridget St John along with Isaac Guillory, who were both very helpful and encouraging.

Bridget was signed to Chrysalis and she was promoting her new album, Jumblequeen.[1] Isaac, an American former member of The Crying Shames, was signed to Atlantic Records and was promoting his debut album. I'd seen a guy on the Old Grey Whistle Test who'd struck me as brilliant and it wasn't until we were halfway through the tour that I realised it had been Isaac. He was one of the most astonishingly gifted acoustic guitarists.

Isaac told me how his manager had rung him, telling him, "Don't ask any questions, just get down to this studio right away." When he arrived, there was a tall black guy playing guitar left-handed, he'd only just arrived in England from America, and Isaac rolled them a joint. Normally Isaac would have jammed all night with him, but he was in a hurry to get to a gig. He listened for a short time and then excused himself.

He found out later it was Jimi Hendrix.

There were the three of us and a sound-man in two vehicles. Isaac had his van and I usually travelled with him. I'd spend the journey rolling joints and the cab would be full of smoke. I didn't really need to smoke; I'd be stoned just on the fumes. Bridget had her classic old sixties Rover and when we arrived at one university and someone asked her, "Are you Buffy Saint Marie?" she answered "Yes." Isaac, a consummate professional, insisted that we change our guitar strings for every gig; I wasn't going to be making much money from the tour, so the string changing proved expensive. Isaac had a magical touch on the guitar and taught me a few technical things, but mostly I learned just from absorbing his playing and the way his voice worked against his guitar. He'd done an acoustics course and could go into a room and, be-

*At the King's Road Theatre, supporting Kilburn and the High Roads
(Ian Dury's band)*

tween him and the sound-man, assess exactly how to create a perfect sound.

We all had places in London. I was living in Barnes with Julie at the time. If we were in the north, we'd stay at Park Lodge, Ripley. In Derbyshire we'd stay at Bridget's house in Sparrowpit. It was on an isolated row of cottages on the side of a hill in the Peak District. One night she put on a Jackson Browne album. I'd not heard him before; he was my age and he set the bar high. For Everyman was a revelation and since then I've always loved his songs.

I'd open the show, then it would be Isaac's set and I'm sure glad I didn't have to follow him. Being Bridget's tour, she was on last and finally the three of us would perform an encore together. There were two Dylan songs and which one we did, depended on whether there was a piano for me to play. If there was, Bridget would sing Just Like a Woman, which received an excellent review in the Times. If there was no piano, we'd play All Along the Watch-

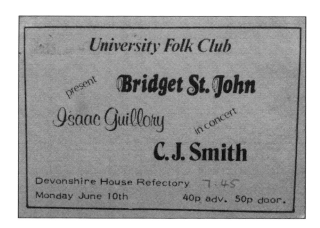

University Folk Club

present **Bridget St. John**

Isaac Guillory *in concert*

C. J. Smith

Devonshire House Refectory 7·45
Monday June 10th   40p adv. 50p door.

tower, in which we each sang a verse. Isaac showed me the rhythm guitar part he wanted me to play and then he played some amazing lead over it.

Bridget was scheduled to do a session for The Old Grey Whistle Test with Bob Harris. She'd booked the rhythm section from Steeleye Span to accompany her and Isaac would play guitar, so I went along with them. The studio was surprising[y small and I stood in the control room behind the glass. Now I can imagine the original Wailers in there doing Stir It Up, a clip I never tire of. Steeleye's bass man, Rick Kemp, had a cool jacket that Bridget had embroidered beautifully with roses and leaves. She offered to embroider the back of my blue denim jacket, which kept her busy for the rest of the tour. The jacket looked even better as it faded.

Towards the end of the tour, we rolled up at one of the London universities. The university crowds had been appreciative and enthusiastic throughout the tour but tonight was different. Walking on stage I felt an unease in the audience. Isaac followed and from the wings, I noticed some arguments break out. One guy stood up and shouted across the room. Heated words were exchanged, fingers pointed.

Bridget's songs were mainly hearth and home, full of peaceful insight, delivered with her gentle charm. But by now the audience were unusually restless. Isaac and I were standing in the wings on opposite sides of the stage. Bridget started into the title track of her new album, Jumblequeen, and she only got as far as the line, "Flying to Belfast, flags are at half-mast" when the place erupted. Suddenly fists were flying and in front of the stage, a big pile of bodies were wrestling, thumping, kicking and screaming at each other. Empty beer glasses were being thrown, one missing Bridget's head by inches, hitting the wall at the back of the stage. Instinctively, Isaac and I rushed to the two microphones on either side of Bridget, trying to calm things down. Glasses were still flying and our pleas for calm were largely ignored in the en-

Isaac Guillory

suing riot. Eventually the fighting and threats subsided and nervously, Bridget finished her set. No one explained what it had been about and we all needed a stiff drink after that.

Isaac was an extraordinarily handsome, charismatic young man and he had a following of adoring teenage girls. Four of them had followed the tour from town to town, so one night, Isaac invited them back to the house where we were staying. Folk musicians on tour are traditionally invited to stay either with the venue organiser or with someone who has a big house and genuinely enjoys the company of dope fiends and crazy alcoholics. Believe me, I've known folk musicians who can easily out-drink and out-drug most rock musicians. They are notorious in many respects and in Isaac's case, teenage fans did not go home dissatisfied. One at a time, his teenage fan-club were led out of the living room into the adjoining bedroom and then eventually, all four young women returned to the party in various states of disarray. Bridget was horrified - after all he was a married man with a family. I behaved impeccably of course and took note that this is the kind of thing that can easily happen if you take too many handsome pills.

After the tour, Isaac invited me to his family home to spend a weekend in the country, recording some of my songs with him in his home studio. It was very good of him to spend the time but his wife didn't agree. Unknown to me, she resented him spending the entire weekend recording and the second day, there was an enormous row upstairs in their bedroom, which I assumed had been brewing for some time. It culminated in her throwing something and consequently, breaking the bedroom window. Isaac and I had to make a quick escape. We drove into the nearest town, found an Indian restaurant and waited for things to calm down while we planned our future. The previous night, we'd seen Leo Sayer on TV dressed as a clown. Isaac turned to me and said, "Don't let them do that to us whatever happens." We wouldn't.

It was the first stirrings of the punk era and the times they were a-changing again and fast. From the music papers, to the major record companies, no one was interested in New Bob Dylans any more. Bridget and Isaac were suddenly told they'd lost their recording contracts and word came from Chrysalis that they were not going to sign me. The fact that Atlantic had dropped Isaac seemed like a huge mistake to me. He might never have been a million seller but he was a class act who would have attracted a world-wide fan-base and gathered longevity.

I can remember sitting alone in a pub, pondering recent events and coming to terms with the fact that, if I was being honest with myself, I didn't really know what I was doing. I simply wasn't strong enough on my own and I knew I didn't have that burning desire to become rich and famous. The truth was, from what I'd seen, I'd become apprehensive and rather frightened of the very idea.

At the same time, it didn't mean I was going to be diverted from my life-long compulsion to write songs and play music. It did put a big dent in my confidence though for a long time. You get one shot at the title and if you don't have it together, or you don't have that sheer sense of destiny, forget it.

Many years later Isaac was booked to play in my home town and I persuaded the organisers to book me and my band on the same bill. It was a very successful night and it was great to connect with him again. Isaac had previously, only seen me play solo, which wasn't my forte, so I was glad he

could see me with my band. I wasn't tempted to perform solo again for many years. I like being in a band, I like the banter and the camaraderie. I've been in bands almost all of my life since my teens. It's my social life as well, hopefully with a bunch of like-minded people, and I like that feeling of being part of a gang - us against the world.

68

Penguins (The Price of Fame)

It was about lunchtime when I ran into Brian May outside Kensington Market. It had been a while since I'd seen him so I suggested we go for a drink. He said he had to take a copy of his new album, Sheer Heart Attack to some friends who had a stall in the market, so I tagged along. The pub behind the market was packed. I walked in first with Brian following close behind. The hubbub of noise from the lunchtime crowd suddenly stopped dead. It was as if someone had switched the volume off. Everyone was staring at us, some with their mouths wide open.

Luckily a corner seat was just being vacated to the right of the door. I indicated to Brian to sit there and made my way to the bar. Pushing through the crowd, I could hear people muttering under their breath, "Is that the guy from Queen?" "Who's this guy?" I ordered two pints of beer and made my way back to the corner seat. By this time the hubbub had gradually returned. Though no one had approached Brian, he was still the object of everyone's attention and it was apparent that a gap had formed between him and the crowd. People were trying to appear unconcerned whilst still occasionally sneaking glances. I sat down. He said no one had bought him a pint for years, they always expected him to buy the drinks. I told him his was the next round.

Brian was living on Queensway, which seemed appropriate, in a basement flat with his girlfriend. He'd just arrived back from Queen's first tour of Japan where, to their surprise, at the airport, they'd had a Beatles' reception. He showed me his bathroom; there was fungus growing on the damp walls. He was broke and pissed off coming back to this after the success of the Japanese tour. (It later conspired that Queen's management was ripping them off, driving around in fancy cars.)

Brian showed me four small dolls a Japanese fan had made. They were dressed in silk with every detail including the faces of the four of them were exquisite, perfectly reproduced in every way. He took me into a back room which was full of stuffed penguins, all sent by fans; just inside the door were small penguins, getting increasingly bigger until you got to a huge penguin in the corner of the back wall, almost reaching the ceiling. I asked him, "What's with the penguins?" He said the other three had things the fans knew they liked, fast cars, Japanese furniture and who knows what John Deacon was into. Put on the spot in an interview, Brian couldn't think of anything so he said he liked penguins. Consequently, by the end of the tour, they'd had to order an extra limo just for the penguins.

69

Surrender to the Rhythm

In 1971, on our first night in the big city, I'd taken Johnny and Andy to my local, the West Kensington. In my absence it had become a pub rock venue for bands like Ducks Deluxe and Bees Make Honey and that night it just happened to be Brinsley Schwarz who were playing. They had a guest singer who sang Van Morrison's Wild Night. I looked at Johnny and Andy and I'm sure they were thinking the same as me; if this is the standard of the average band here, we might as well go home. As it turned out, the singer was the greatest British white blues singer ever to draw breath; Frankie Miller and the Brinsleys were easily the finest band on the pub circuit.

Three years later, in 1974, I was the song writer and front man in Big Black Sedan. Chrysalis Records did the usual record company trick - pick out the main man and ditch the rest of the band. (Their logic was, it's easier to deal with one guy than four, resulting in a lot of dreams being washed away and hearts broken.) I immediately felt at a loss. It wasn't as much fun on my own and I needed a band, so I called Johnny. Although he'd gone back up north, he agreed to come down to London when required.

We needed a rhythm section for recording and so we approached Nicky Lowe and Billy Rankin from the Brinsleys. Apart from playing bass and being the front man, the first thing you noticed about Nicky Lowe was that he was extremely cool. He had a pullover with the tune of Surrender to the Rhythm (their best- known song) written all the way round in notation. His later solo album title, Jesus of Cool, said it all. They invited us to Beaconsfield to a farmhouse they shared, where we arrived on a Saturday morning and Nicky and Billy were up early, waiting for us. They were full of excitement because the previous weekend, there'd been a knock on the door and, when they opened it, lo and behold, there on the doorstep stood Robbie Robertson and Levon Helm of The Band. They explained that they'd heard Brinsley Schwartz' records, had found their address through their management and asked to come and stay for a few days. The rest of The Band then arrived and soon the two bands were set up in the big kitchen. Nicky said Bob Andrews, their organist could hardly believe he was there picking Garth Hudson's brains. It must have felt like Christmas.

Johnny and I arrived the morning after The Band had left. Brinsley's gear was still set up in the kitchen so we plugged in and, as we were playing, the other three Brinsleys wandered into the kitchen. Bob Andrews, Brinsley and Ian Gomm made themselves toast and tea and, still in their dressing gowns, Brinsley and Ian put on their guitars. Bob sat at the organ and they joined in. We thought, this is the right way to do it, all living under the same roof, playing and writing music together like The Band at Big Pink.

When we had a tea-break, Nicky took me into the barn next door and there, propped strategically against a stall was his orange Chet Atkins Gretsch Country Gentleman. What a vision; the brown barn with just that beautiful orange guitar resting there. He explained that it was for sale. I picked it up, it played good and when I turned it over, it had a big cushion pad on the back for extra comfort. He wanted three hundred quid for it and I didn't have that much in my back pocket at the time. Now of course, you could put a nought on the end of that, at least.

Johnny and I never did follow up the idea of recording with Billy and Nicky, partly due to my crisis of confidence, and, in any case, shortly after, Paul McCartney asked them to be the support band on his British tour.

Brinsley's roadie, John, told me this story; Ian Gomm like so many of us, had been brought up on the Beatles' music and on the tour, him and Macca would sit around playing Beatles' songs. Sometimes Paul would forget the chords, even though he'd written the songs but Ian knew them all and would put him right.

70

Boxes

Johnny Vincent said to me recently that the extent of our ambition in London was to be Brindsley Schwartz, the British equivalent of The Band, and he was right. It was never about world domination, we just wanted to have a good creative band that we could be proud of. Although genuinely obsessed with music, neither of us had that burning need to become rich and famous. I'd only recently realised that if you're not confident and self-assured, fame can be a pie in the face. Dylan said in an interview that a kid might have the looks and the voice but if he doesn't have the experience, he won't make it.

I was reminded, at college Freddie had printed the words The Experience in coloured letters on glossy white card and handed them out to various people for no apparent reason.

If we're talking about street smarts, I still didn't have enough experience.

I'd seen how Queen was a band which, between the four of them, had what it takes, so I wasn't fooling myself any longer. They knew what they were doing whereas I didn't even know who I was. It was evident that I had potential but I knew I was a long way from fulfilling that potential. I certainly wasn't strong enough to make it on my own and I'm a team player anyway. I enjoy bouncing ideas off other people and without the reassurance of the other guys, my confidence was slipping away. I'd become very uncertain about my relationship to the music business. If you don't know how you want to be presented, people will manipulate you and try to mould you into something you might not be comfortable with.

I was starting to realise, there are a lot of boxes to tick if you're going to make it in rock n' roll; you have to be determined and confident in your own talent and the talents of everyone in your band. Be aware that you make your own luck. (Your front-man having a strong sense of destiny that he's going to be a superstar certainly helps.) You need to know who you are and be clear about what you're doing. You need to be something of a socialite and an op-portunist and be available to attend the right parties. Remember the names of secretaries and record company people and try to learn about the business side. Find a good manager who genuinely loves your music and is prepared to do whatever it takes, within the law, to promote you.

In retrospect it's easy to say, I know that now. You're going to find out fairly quickly if you can do all this and if you can't, you have to accept that being a rock n' roll star isn't meant to be. Maybe it's time to think about doing something else. It's a tough realisation.

> *"All of the old faces, they ask you why you're back.*
> *They fit you with position and the keys to your daddy's Cadillac.*
> *In the darkness of your room, your mother calls you by your true name. You*
> *remember the faces, the places, the names.*
> *You know it's never over, it's relentless as the rain."*

Bruce Springsteen – Adam Raised a Cain[1]

Part Three

71

The Zephyrs

After the university tour, I left London disillusioned with the music business but now at least I didn't have to concern myself with talk of hit singles or the latest fad any more. At the Robsons', good friends of mine in Ripley, I met the guitarist Roger Harrison, known to his friends as Dodger. He invited me down to Hunslet, a less salubrious part of Leeds, where he lived in a house on the edge of a new motorway extension they were building. The house was run down with holes in the walls and he took me into the cellar where there was a piano and an impressive wall of amps and speaker cabinets. It turned out that most of them were either empty or beyond repair but then, I was in a bad state of repair myself and I really needed to find a new life and a different musical direction.

The first thing Dodger did was get me stoned. He had a pipe made from a cardboard tube, about three feet long and three inches in diameter. The bowl was a hole at the far end with silver foil which he loaded with resin. Once lit, it blew your head off. It was like going up in a lift. "Doing the tube," as it became known, became a ritual before we went down to the cellar to jam. Dodger was heavily into Carlos Santana. He looked like a cross between James Dean and Robbie Robertson and he made me laugh so much that I stayed for over a week. Finding a new friendship is always great fun but it's not often you realise you've found a buddy and that's very special. You don't find too many of those in a lifetime.

He soon introduced me to his friend and former tutor from Bradford Art School, Martin Radige. Martin was a little guy with a black moustache who looked a lot like Ringo Starr. He had a wacky sense of humour and played the bass, so before long it began to dawn on me, we were starting a band. Richard Bostock was a medical student who was soon to drop out of medical college. Richard (stage name – Alphonse Material) was tall, good looking, politically radical, loved be-bop and had long brown hair down to his waist. He played tenor sax, shared our surreal sense of humour and would soon become an essential part of our new-found brotherhood, soon to be known as The Zephyrs.

Big Kev, who worked as an electrician for the coal board, was a friend of Dodger's and would often join us, smoking and jamming late into the night. Kev didn't have an instrument but sometimes would be inspired to join in on mouth trumpet like a trad jazz trumpeter. Sometimes Kev would be our roadie. He's a huge guy with massive hands and the constitution of an ox, often staying up all night smoking, going to work the next day and then doing the same thing the following night.

Roger "Dodger" Harrison (stage name – Roger Rock-a-While)

We didn't have a regular drummer but Andy Moss came along. One day there was a sharp rap on the cellar window. Andy put his drumsticks down carefully on his snare drum and, walking over to the window, announced, "It's the Rozzers." For several seconds no one moved, then suddenly panic descended. Dope was dropped into holes in walls, flushed down the toilet, swallowed in mind-dissolving quantities. Dodger opened the door with a fixed smile and wide eyes. Amazingly, they hadn't come to complain about the noise and weren't about to bust us. They just happened to be looking for an address and they went on their way much to our relief.

Phil Taylor, (later known as Animal Phil Taylor) lived nearby. He was sixteen and moved his see-through drumkit into the cellar. He would arrive and practice on his own or, if we were already down there, he would join in. If he was already playing, we would go down there and jam along to whatever he was doing. I don't remember saying more than a few words to him. His mum (who worked on Lewis' cheese counter) would sometimes bring him sandwiches if he'd been there playing for hours, in case he'd forgotten to eat. Legend has it that he hitched a lift to London from Lemmy but I don't know how much truth there is in that. Phil was a wild boy, as you may know, and he turned up one day with a car load of class A drugs which he asked to stash in the house. He told Dodger he'd been raided by the police so he'd swallowed everything he had. He'd then stolen a car and driven from London to Leeds. How he drove we will never know but he was out of his mind by the time he arrived. Presumably he'd stopped off to replace his lost provisions. I left it to Dodger to decide what to do; it was his place after all and I didn't ask any questions.

Dodger, Martin and I paid Phil a visit when we were in London. He shared a first floor flat with an assortment of wild looking punks. Phil was sitting on a black plastic sofa, wearing black jeans, stripped to the waist, when a large bluebottle landed on his chest. He didn't notice it but the three of us did and it seemed significant enough that we all remarked on it as we emerged back onto street level. It was immediately evident that there were several police squad cars surrounding the building.

Dave became our drummer for a while. He looked the part, straight dark hair and a moustache. He was a nice guy and could have passed for one of the Eagles. There was a lot of dope, far too much in fact, and a fair amount of drinking in The Fenton near Leeds University. It was the mid-seventies and, if you were a musician, it was par for the course. At the same time, I'd found a bunch of great characters who were a lot of fun. I was aware that I needed to find a way of making a living and Dodger showed great generosity giving me a roof over my head and a job, assisting him silk-screening mirrors working in the basement of a house on Meanwood Ridge.

The mirror business was a boom market in pub mirrors, reproducing old pub signs, Coca Cola ads, Art Nouveau and Art Deco designs. It was a fad that lasted for a few years until finally the market was saturated. It was an interesting time as the local gangsters had seized the opportunity to muscle in and take over the business. Ex art students, such as us, could be seen fraternizing in pubs with gangsters who distributed the mirrors for a substantial cut. On a Friday we might be supplying one guy and then on the Monday, we'd be informed we were now supplying someone else because there'd been a gun fight over the weekend.

Mick, who did the artwork, seemed like a gentle enough guy. He certainly didn't look like he ought to be mixing with ruffians, he appeared far too effeminate, though he was a big fella.

One Saturday night we met Mick out on the town. He was dressed in a perfectly tailored, bright green silk suit. Dodger said to me "Look at Mick's hands." He had fists like hams. Apparently, Mick and his mate would make a point of going to the roughest pubs in Hunslet and Beeston, where they would camp it up until some homophobes would pick a fight. Then Mick and his mate would take them outside and beat the shit out of them. I never looked at Mick in the same way again and I think he found my recent enlightenment quite amusing.

Richard and Martin were occasionally brought in to help with the mirrors if we had a big order. The glass would be stacked against a wall with clothes-pegs between each sheet of glass. Considering that we were stoned much of the time, it's a wonder there weren't any accidents. One of the jobs we had was to print Mucha's Four Seasons; we were printing Autumn that particular day and, after smoking a J, we decided to blend the colours with vignettes, to make them look more like the Mucha original. It was a long print run and when we'd finished, we were well pleased. We thought our crime bosses would be similarly delighted with the improved results. They sent them back the next day, with instructions to scrape them off, start again and this time do them properly.

Richard and Martin were into what Captain Beefheart described as "opaque melodies that would bug most people."[1] We all became fans of the Magic Band. Martin had taught drawing at Bradford Art College. He'd built glass fronted wooden boxes with assemblages like the artist Joseph Cornell. We all shared a Surrealistic sense of humour but Martin was a master of the art and could make insane comments that would crack everyone up. Richard loved bebop, especially Thelonious Monk and Charley Mingus. He played tenor sax and double bass. Dodger, an ex-mod, was a soul-man through and through. I was the bluesman.

When I phoned Dodger recently to check a few facts, I quoted John Prine,

"Pulling when you ought to be shoving."[2] I was referring to us pulling in different musical directions instead of pushing our musical influences together to make our own stew out of it. If a band has its own sound, it can do almost anything. It can embrace many different styles, giving it scope, which I always wanted. Some bands remain one-dimensional, but I wanted us to develop and improve.

Dodger is a natural leader and he took the bull by the horns, pointing us in a soul direction, which made a lot of sense as we needed a main focus. Before I met him, he'd been over to Manchester to see Little Feat and Tower of Power, so it was Little Feat for me, and Tower of Power for Dodger, that became major influences. Tower of Power was a musician's band - they never really caught on with the general public. They were slick and jazz-influenced; perhaps it was too complex for general pop culture ears. We tried to emulate the slickness of Tower of Power, but in retrospect it wasn't really us. Maybe it was a mistake, but at least we did try to do something difficult, be it beyond our capabilities. It's exciting to make that reach and push the boundaries sometimes and, like the Tower of Power song says, we were "Willing to Learn." I was happy that these guys had propelled me into a different mindset and expanded my musical horizons since leaving London. I'd so needed to make that change.

The Zephyrs' first gig was at the Majestic Hotel in Harrogate. It was an inauspicious start as we were only a few songs into the first set, when a blue arm, that turned out to be the long arm of the law, reached across and grabbed my microphone. I watched as Richard's saxophone was promptly pulled out of his mouth and soon, the place was swarming with uniformed police who obviously had nothing better to do that night. They'd had a complaint, presumably from one of the hotel guests, and the officer in charge then announced that they were closing down the show. So, we were off to a flying start and, when word got around, it proved great publicity. I'm only sorry they didn't arrest us.

I was friends with a couple who lived in Pateley Bridge, Jean and Don, (not their real names). Don was very keen for the Zephyrs to move there. He offered to manage the sales side of a mirror business. He'd designed a mirror commemorating the upcoming '76 American Bicentennial. It was an impressive design and he planned to sell them through the American Base at Menwith Hill. (In retrospect I think he just wanted some mates around.) He hatched a plan to rent Gouthwaite House, a farmhouse with spectacular views of Gouthwaite reservoir and the surrounding hills. There was a barn next to the house, big enough to rehearse at one end and set up the silk-screen bed at the other end. Naively I was taken with the idea of "getting it together in the country" and I put it to the Zephyrs. Dodger, like me, is a country boy at heart. He grew up on a remote farm on the Pennines, in Rochdale, so I took him up to visit and he was immediately sold on the plan. Martin and Richard were soon persuaded that it was a good move and with help from several friends, including Big Kev, we relocated lock, stock and barrel to the country.

Martin, Richard and myself moved into Gouthwaite House, along with my two friends. Don would do the artwork and sell the mirrors, Jean would do the cooking, we would do the chores, print the mirrors, compose and play music. It seemed like the perfect set-up. What could possibly go wrong?

Dodger and his girlfriend, Cherry, moved into the flat over the bank in the town.

We set up the silk screen bed and the musical equipment in the barn and as soon as we started playing, the trouble started. We were miles from anywhere, several fields away from our nearest neighbour and it took one song before they rang to complain about the noise. We had thought we'd be welcomed with open arms by the locals but we couldn't have been more wrong. This was not an artistic community. This was not The Band moving to Woodstock as I'd envisioned. This was more like moving into redneck country, with all the ingrained right-wing prejudices thrown in for good measure. This was a North Yorkshire narrow-minded, conservative small town and they hated us. Richard Bostock with his hair down to his waist was named Creeping Jesus by the locals. Eventually he rented himself a caravan to find some privacy and on returning one night found that someone had pushed it over a cliff. That was the final straw for Richard and he was the first to throw in the towel and return to civilisation.

The summer of '76 was a glorious summer and I recall walking miles among the hills and streams. Martin had his little black MG sports car which suited him perfectly. Dodger would drive out to the barn in his classic vintage Hillman Minx in the morning and we'd get to work printing the mirrors and then rehearsing the songs. We found a local drummer, also named Martin, who liked what we were doing though he was younger than us. He had a good feel and could play the funky stuff. About a year later we were shocked to hear he'd died in a car crash on the A1.

Padda Long sported a beard you could have lost a badger in. He was Phil Lynott's cousin and lived across the other side of the reservoir, He played saxophone and various stringed instruments, so now we had a brass section and could sound like a regular soul band when the occasion required.

We played regularly at our local, the Watermill, where there was a big events room. People were curious to know what we were up to so there were regular visitors. Friends, girlfriends, family and musicians would turn up. Tim Staffell and Clive Armitage drove up from London to pay us a visit. Tim sat in with us one night at the Watermill and sang Dylan's I Shall Be Released which seemed very appropriate under the circumstances. We jammed the song for what seemed like an eternity and it felt good playing with Tim again.

Tempers were fraying; Don wasn't keeping up his end of the bargain.

The mirrors weren't selling, money was tight and when someone bought a Sunday newspaper and was accused of squandering money, I reckoned things had gone too far. A couple of people went to London to deliver mirrors and on their return, just happened to mentioned that they'd bought tickets and been to see the Rolling Stones. That was the final straw for me and resentments were bubbling under the surface. To be fair, I'd got us into this mess and I didn't have a clue how to get out of it. I knew there was too much smoking and not enough talking about what the problems were and how to overcome them. Dodger was like a bear with a sore head and not the easiest man to confront when he's that way out so I tended to retreat into myself. How come my life had taken such a wrong turn when two summers ago I was on a university tour, anticipating being signed to a record company? At the same time, I was clearly aware that Queen were conquering the world. Now here I was in the middle of nowhere with no money, with a bunch of guys I'd grown to love dearly, in a band that was sadly, coming apart at the seams. Richard had an expression, no matter how bad things got, he'd say "It's sociologically very interesting." At the end of the summer, the dream of country life had become a hard reality and with Richard's departure, one by one, we made our way back to Leeds.

72

The Amazing Torpedoes

Dodger, being an enterprising guy, found the first floor of a disused factory off Meanwood Road and we moved the silk-screen bed up there. It was the same arrangement as we'd had at Gouthwaite; silk-screen equipment at one end nearest to the door and musical equipment at the far end. Known as The Factory, other bands would rehearse there when we weren't using it, or we would jam with friends. One day, a sixteen-year-old lad arrived; his name was Gary Husband and it was immediately clear to us that he was a phenomenal drummer. We'd had a succession of drummers but never settled on a permanent one so naturally we offered him the job. He told us that he was already committed; he'd agreed to join the Sid Lawrence Orchestra the following week. We loved his playing and eventually he joined Level 42 and then became a much sought-after session drummer.

One day The Zephyrs were rehearsing and Martin appeared distracted, looking out of the window. Walking along the street below was a glamorous young woman wearing a short skirt and a tight bright-red pullover which accentuated her curvaceous figure. "Look at those amazing torpedoes!" he exclaimed.

So that's when we decided to change the name of the band.

The Amazing Torpedoes played Harrogate's Royal Hall supporting The Heavy Metal Kids. Dodger's friend, Simon, was roadying for us, along with Big Kev, and just as we were heading for the stage, I passed Simon standing in the wings. He asked me, "Have you got a harmonica? Can you stick it between my teeth? I'm about to have an epileptic fit." He lay down on the floor and I grabbed a harmonica and stuck it between his teeth as he requested. The Torpedoes had already started the first number, playing an over-long introduction and wondering where the hell their singer was, but there wasn't much I could do except stick with Simon. When he came out of the fit, he looked up at me through glazed eyes and said, "That was amazing!" I immediately ran on stage, stood behind the Hammond and launched into the first song.

Reece Phillips (who had previously played drums for us at the Factory) was into all the latest technology. He would arrive plugging in numerous devices, a radio, a light, a toothbrush, an electric razor, you name it. He was the first person I saw carrying one of those early mobile phones the size of a house brick. His band was on the same bill as us at the Royal Hall.

At the back of the hall was a row of telephone booths; when Reece's band started up, Dodger and I decided to play a trick on him. Dodger manned a telephone while I kept a look out by the door. We waited for Reece to start his drum solo, I gave the signal and Dodger rang him up. The look of sheer confusion and panic on his face was priceless. He didn't have enough hands to answer the phone. We thought he was about to spontaneously combust.

We had a sizable PA (public address) system with huge bass bins and when my Aunty Rene sadly died, she kindly left me a grand, so I bought a decent mixing desk. Leeds Polytechnic hired the PA for a Police gig and I remember we did the PA for a Soft Cell gig in town. I can't say we liked what they were doing but certainly, Mark Almond had star quality. Our PA was booked every week for the F Club, the new punk venue, and I've never in my life felt so old. Here was the first youth movement that, in my late twenties I couldn't be a part of. Siouxsie and the Banshees had future Sex Pistol Sid Vicious on bass; bass low slung, stripped to the waist, spitting onto the crowd who were pogoing like mad and spitting back. The old guard was gone and this felt like alien territory.

Richard Bostock and I teamed up with a friend, Paul Hayes, who performed a magic act sawing his girlfriend Sally in half. He was also a fire eater. He wanted to put a band together for a gig (this could be our Spinal Tap puppet show moment) and it turned out he had a very good bass player, Abell Damagie. Then Dodger joined so now the band was getting good. Later, when Paul Hayes was out of action, we carried on without him and became the house band at the International Club in Chapeltown.

Paul arrived home one day to find a burglar had broken into his flat and was busy unplugging his stereo. The guy panicked and stabbed Paul with a kitchen knife before fleeing the scene. Paul's immediate thought was to hide his dope, so leaving a trail of blood up the stairs, he then phoned Sally and passed out. He was in hospital for some weeks and the first thing he did when he'd recovered, was to book the band for his comeback gig at the Royal Park. The pub was packed. The band played a couple of songs and then Paul appeared on stage juggling knives. He stood back and the three knives suddenly flew up in the air, fell and stuck in the stage. There was a gasp from the audience followed by awed silence and then, tumultuous applause.

Tex Hardin was a Jamaican who lived a couple of doors down from me in Chapeltown and had been one of the first black men to arrive in Leeds.

He told me people would run away from him in fear and he was known as The Blackamoor. Tex was a lovely guy and he introduced us to the West Indian proprietor of Chapeltown's International Club, Lee Hyman. Lee would book us to play regularly, the only condition being that we had to back the strippers on Sunday afternoons. Mercifully this only happened on a couple of occasions but Richard was in his element. He would prowl the front of the stage in his girlfriend's full-length fur coat, with his hair down to his waist, next to the stripper, blowing rude noises on his saxophone. Now, with our West Indian drummer, Terry, we were truly an international band. The club had the stage at one end and pillars down each side of the dancehall behind which were tables where you could sit and socialise. It was a rough place at times, especially at weekends, with people from out of town as well as locals, a lot of working girls and their pimps and a lot of students. It was the centre of the local community, fulfilling a function the church had once provided but with more sex, drugs and rock n' roll. It was dangerous work; we were halfway through our second set when there was a scream and the dancehall cleared rapidly. There was one black guy, I'd say in his mid-fifties, left standing in the middle of the room with his back to us. A knife was sticking out of his back as he staggered the full length of the dancehall to the front door. Richard caught my eye and I knew he meant keep playing no matter what. We didn't see the guy again and everyone resumed dancing as if nothing had happened.

Just another regular Saturday night.

73

May You Never

Mary Gordon was the original punk, before punk was invented. She had a gentle Edinburgh accent, wore plastic jewellery from Woolworths and, on special occasions, a plastic parrot on her shoulder. Celia Chambers was a no- nonsense hippy girl who lived with her boyfriend in the flat downstairs. She was small and feisty with a wicked sense of humour and she had long wavy auburn hair right down to her ass. This might go somewhere towards explaining why the two of them could go to a Jon Martyn concert and come back with Jon Martyn.

It was the late seventies and I was living with Maggie in Chapeltown. It was almost midnight and we already had a few friends round, when they arrived with the famous folk singer in tow. Maggie had three heroes in her life; Bob Dylan, Van Morrison and Jon Martyn. She had to go into the other room to calm down. Jon Martyn made himself at home right away, rifled through my record collection and selected Freddie King's Getting Ready. As I was putting the record on, he built a large spliff, drinks were served and a fine evening was had by all.

Some of us stayed up for the duration and it was early morning before we got to bed. Maggie made him up a bed on the sofa and after very little sleep, we were up for work. Maggie was a school teacher and I was working in a silk- screen factory on Buslingthorpe Lane, producing art work and cutting stencils. It was alright for Jon Martyn; he could sleep in all morning like a proper musician.

The previous evening, we'd smoked all the dope and Jon needed to score, so I took him round to the back door of the International Club. Like at a speakeasy in a gangster film, there was a sliding wooden panel in the door so the doorman could assess the clientele. He recognised me but, of course, failed to recognise the most famous folk singer in the country. He let us in and I sat at a table talking to two West Indian guys, while, within minutes and without any assistance, Jon scored several ounces of the very best Moroccan Island Records' money could buy.

In the course of the evening's conversation, Jon would take on multiple personalities. He would suddenly become Scottish, with a thick Glasgow accent. Then he'd turn into a Cockney barrow boy, or a posh boy who'd obviously been to Eton. These were integrated parts of his personality which he enjoyed immensely. There was also the sensitive and gentle poet who you imagine he really is (or would like to be), when you listen to his music. I sensed there was a conflict going on there which probably gave him his edge. Though I'm not a psychiatrist, some people really are crazy.

Never meet your heroes. After four days and nights, Jon Martyn had worn us out. We waved him off, with some relief, down the street. As he disappeared round the corner Maggie turned to me and said, "If ever Bob Dylan or Van Morrison come knocking on the door, tell them to fuck off."

74

The John Dyson Band

Every musician who has ever known John Dyson will have John Dyson stories to tell. There are enough John Dyson stories to fill a book. I have to say, he was a rather unpleasant character, grossly overweight with a bunch of issues you wouldn't care to delve into too deeply. John lived with his mother, a stout, matronly woman who was a retired school teacher. In spite of his problems (or more likely because of them) not unlike Eric Clapton, he'd been driven to become a fine guitarist who occasionally produced moments of astonishing brilliance. He'd started learning guitar young and by the early sixties, was backing ska and early Reggae singers, like Desmond Decker. Then he'd played in the house band at Batley Variety Club, working with Neil Sedaka and other stars of the fifties and early sixties.

John was a school teacher by day, so at my first rehearsal in his mother's front room, he gave out chord sheets he'd carefully prepared and went through each song, pointing out the changes in detail as though we were a bunch of six- year-olds. He had his Dansette record player set up and when it came to his guitar solo, he dropped the needle onto the record at precisely the right place and announced, "This is what I shall be playing."

Before every gig, John was a nervous wreck, chain smoking and downing several pints of beer. Then, before we went on stage, he would come round all the band members and ask if we'd been to the toilet (clearly a feature of his teaching practice.) "Yes John," we would all reply, dead pan.

John had several classic guitars, yet for some perverse reason he would turn up with some plank of wood, suggesting it was every bit as good as any top of the range Gibson. After a first set one night, perhaps feeling his playing wasn't quite up to scratch, he decided to call it a day.

"All this gear is for sale," he suddenly announced to the audience. "I'm selling everything." We eventually managed to calm him down before the second set. He used to say," We're just rock players, we're only half talented." Johnny Vincent and I still remind each other of this fact, whenever we might be in danger of getting too big for our boots.

Mike Reed, the drummer, was a big fella; over six feet tall with receding black hair. Seated behind his drums, he looked like the Buddha. During the customary drum solo, Mike would stand up and walk all the way around his drum-kit, still hitting things, and, on completing the circle, return to his drum- stool. This had always proved a hit with the club audiences. On this particular night, Mike had perhaps had a little too much to drink and we were playing on a sloping stage. Arriving at the customary drum solo, Mike stood up, got half way round the kit and promptly fell headlong into the drums. Various drums were sent in all directions. The cymbal stands and cymbals came crashing to the stage. Our leader was busy singing at the front of the stage, oblivious to the ensuing calamity. At that moment a cymbal sliced his microphone lead and his voice was suddenly silenced, much to his astonishment. The perplexed look on John's face as he turned round was a sight to behold. Drums were now rolling down the sloping stage and Mike finished up lying on his back hugging his floor-tom to his chest. The audience was now on its feet applauding. They thought it was part of the act. The bass player Steve and I witnessed the whole thing and were doubled up, helpless with laughter. Would we be able to replicate this dazzling performance on successive nights? It would take some serious rehearsal.

I was still working my day job in the art department at the silk-screen factory on Buslingthorpe Lane when I decided to take up the offer to join the John Dyson Band. I wasn't making much money so it was purely a commercial decision. They played pubs but mainly worked the South Yorkshire Working Men's Clubs, playing the hits of the day. One of the few highlights for me was a chance to sing Stevie Wonder's Living in the City. There was Peter Frampton's big hit, Show Me the Way but otherwise, the set list was mostly cheese - pure Stilton in fact. Every club looked exactly the same; for all I knew the audience might well have been the same crowd. There was usually a "turn" on before us, sometimes a singer, accompanied by a drummer and an organist. (Some clubs still had a full-sized Hammond organ with a set of bass pedals.) At half time, everything stopped for the tombola, the club chairman or someone drawing ping-pong balls with numbers on from a Perspex barrel; "Legs eleven, two fat ladies - eighty eight, on its own - number one." If you've ever seen Peter Kay's Phoenix Nights, you get the picture.

I wasn't really thinking about my singing, just on tramlines most of the time. I wasn't particularly trying and that's when I discovered my own voice. Not that I couldn't sing before but I found a distinctive sound. It had been there all along, the clue is in the way you talk. It can be the hardest thing to find. Mick Jagger sounded like Mick Jagger at eighteen. Johnny Vincent told me the hardest thing for a guitarist is finding your own sound. Hats off to Jeff Beck, Hank Marvin and to Mark Knopfler, who only has to play one note for you to know who he is. It's strange, just when you stop trying too hard and drop any pretence, that you can discover something fundamental.

Fundamental to John Dyson was food. He could win an eating competition. He could systematically eat his way into the history books. One night after a gig we went for a curry. (It's always been a tradition, ever since the sixties with the Liberty Takers, if a band is playing anywhere in or around Bradford, Yorkshire's curry capital, to go for a curry.) Maggie was with me and being an ardent feminist, John's misogynistic views garnered little sympathy. Consequently, by the end of the meal, the two of them ended up nose to nose, screaming at each other across the restaurant table, the ensuing journey back to Leeds producing a somewhat uncomfortable silence. John, now desperately in need of comfort food, had to stop at a fish and chip shop where I watched him devour a full portion of fish and chips with scraps and curry sauce. Then, still in need of more comfort food, we had to stop again at a hot-dog stand.

He's dead then.

Some years later Tim Lyttle told me John Dyson used to pull this stunt on him but at the time I thought it was just me. He would come to my gigs and stand right in the middle at the front as we went on stage. Then immediately we started playing he would turn his back on the band and start a conversation with whoever was behind him in the audience.

He was irritating and obnoxious at times, never-the-less, musically, he taught me a lot and at least, now I know to pay a visit to the toilet before going on stage, without being told.

75

Dennis and the Dope Plants

D ennis got busted. He had two very large dope plants and the police confiscated both of them. Maybe because the plants were so big, they left them on the steps, outside the back door of the police station and somebody nicked then. The charges were dropped and Dennis got off scott free.

One night, Dennis and I sat up drinking late into the night swapping rock n' roll stories. He told me that in the sixties he was a good friend of Peter Green, of Fleetwood Mac. Green was a socialist and, considering his new found wealth and fame, still chose to live in a fairly modest house. Dennis and Peter were having breakfast one morning when Peter's phone rang; he answered the phone, then came back to the table to finish his bacon and eggs. He didn't say anything so Dennis asked him who rang. "Oh, it was B.B.King, he wants us to go down to a recording session in London." So off they went in Green's two-seater sports car. When they arrived at B.B.King's recording session, Eric Clapton, Dave Mason, everyone and his mother were there. The session soon turned into something of a party. Dennis had taken along his beautifully hand painted Gibson Les Paul. (In recent years it featured in an article in Guitarist magazine.)

Some months earlier Peter Green had decided he needed a cello. As it happened, Dennis had taken some cello lessons as a child, so knew the rudiments and would be able to give the great guitarist some pointers. After all, we all have to start somewhere. They made their purchase at a West End music shop and Dennis managed, with great difficulty, to squeeze the cello between his knees as Green drove through central London, with Dennis hanging on to the cumbersome instrument, now sticking straight up out of the open-top car.

Green mastered the cello in no time (thanks to Dennis's expert tuition I've no doubt) and became good enough to play all the cello parts on his next recording.

Dennis told me that, when Peter Green was at the height of his fame, they were invited to a banquet at Friar Park, George Harrison's house. They drove through the gates and down a long drive to arrive at the house; a Gothic monstrosity that George saved when it was in danger of being demolished, spending years lovingly restoring the house and gardens. A lot of expensive cars were parked by the house when they arrived. They were shown into a Baronial Hall, complete with minstrel gallery and minstrels. The tables were arranged as though for a wedding, with King George sitting in the centre at the top table. Various rock and roll luminaries, including some of the Rolling Stones, were also seated at the top table.

Peter Green and Dennis were seated down the far end of one of the side tables. After the meal, they were summoned to the top table. They sat opposite George, who said to Peter Green, "We'd like to offer you a recording contract with Apple Records."

Green asked, "What's the advance?"

George replied, "There isn't one, it's the privilege of being on Apple Records." Green said, "Come on Dennis, we're off."

Perhaps in retrospect it was a hasty decision.........

Dennis has a cousin who became a big rock star. A letter arrived telling him to go to Leeds City Station, to collect a parcel; it was an Eric Clapton signature Fender Strat, a very welcome gift from his cousin, Chris Rea. Dennis also received a backstage pass for his cousin's upcoming concert at Wembley Stadium. The back stage officials were fairly offhand with Dennis who's a no-nonsense northerner. After the concert, Chris Rea came off stage and the two of them spent the remainder of the evening laughing and joking at the bar and reminiscing about their childhood. The next night Dennis returned with another backstage pass, to find everyone was all over him; "Would you like a drink, Dennis? Perhaps a line of something? Have you met Mandy?"

76

My Favourite Beatle

Chrysalis gave me two tickets for an Alvin Lee concert at the Rainbow. I knew Julie wouldn't be interested so I called my pal Clive. The tickets were for the V.I.P. section. Rod Stewart was right behind us in the queue. I didn't suppose he'd recognise me though I'd met him seven years before with the Steam Packet. Apart from seeing him play in '67 with Jeff Beck, I'd seen him in the early sixties, playing harmonica with the Five Dimensions. Now he was on top of the world with the Faces and his solo career.

We got to our seats which were numbered. Just my luck to get seated behind some hippy with long brown hair down over his shoulders. He had such big hair, I had to strain my neck to peer round him to see the stage. I couldn't help but notice though, seated to his right, in front of Clive, was a stunning blond. I'm ashamed to say, I remember thinking to myself, "What's she doing with this hippy?" When the lights went up at the end of the concert, the hippy stood up and turned around to put on his coat; it was George Harrison. His wife, Patty, was the stunning blond. Clive said, "Hello George." He said hello back but you almost expected him to say "Hello Clive," because you felt like you knew him.

77

The King Bees

The King Bees' origins go all the way back to our early teens. Around 1964 my best friend, David Hudson, was the lead singer in Peter and the Wolves. Pete Knights and Stu Pickersgill were the guitarists. My school friend, Duffy, played bass and Ian Atkinson (Acky) was their drummer. They rehearsed in Dave's grandma's attic, two doors down from where Dave lived, just around the corner from me. He would say to his dad, "I'm just going upstairs to change," to which his dad would unhesitatingly reply, "It's time you did."

One day I suggested to Acky that I paint their band name on the skin of his bass drum. After some consideration he replied, "It's alright, I'll do it myself."

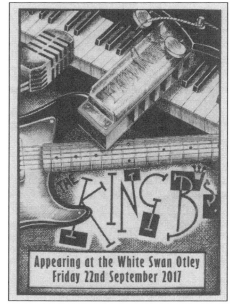

A King Bees poster by Chris Broughton

The next week I saw that, scrawled in blue Biro, about seven inches long, off centre and at an angle of approximately thirty-five degrees, a schoolboy hand had written - Peter and the Wolves. Dave did his best Mick Jagger, bless him, shaking his maracas, pouting and thrusting his pelvis forward with his hands on his hips. They were soon off to an auspicious start.

Johnny Vincent invited me down to his woodshed in Pool where he and his mate, Tony Ridealgh, (later of the Liberty Takers) were trying to start a band. I turned them down because, frankly, they were crap. Their first gig was at the Rugby Club. They only knew Louie Louie and played it for twenty minutes before the singer, Wilky, finally turned up drunk. As they didn't know any more songs, they repeated it, with the interesting addition of slurred vocal accompaniment.

A couple of years later I saw Johnny doing a convincing impression of

his hero, Eric Clapton and was suitably impressed. He was bending those blues notes perfectly and I could see he had real talent. He'd formed the Sons of Sin with drummer Andy Thornton, Stu, Duffy, and Brian Ellison on lead vocals. (You'll remember the Liberty Takers had stolen Brian from them before we became Ellison's Hogline.) In the summer of '67 I formed the East West / Paul Butterfield tribute band with Stu, Duffy, Johnny and Andy.

That summer Kenny Everett was on the radio interviewing the Beatles in an exclusive, featuring some of the soon to be released tracks from Sgt Pepper's Lonely Hearts Club Band. Kenny was on top form and in total awe at having all four Beatles in the studio. I recorded the show on my Phillips reel to reel tape recorder and invited the band round. We sat in my folks' front room, amazed at the scope and inventiveness of the Beatles' new songs. It was like the moon landing. It was that important.

In the late seventies, Johnny, Des, Andy Thornton and myself formed the King Bees. So, it's a family tree going all the way back to the days when we first became interested in guitars and bands. Through the years many of us might have been in several bands at the same time, often out of financial necessity. So rather than being a permanent band, the King Bees would reform and disband from time to time. When we do reappear, people who we haven't seen since the seventies turn out to see us and we always like to play a bunch of those old Chuck Berry and Buddy Holly songs we started out playing as teenagers.

The King Bees. L-R; Johnny Vincent, Andy Thornton, Des O'Hara and CJ

78

The Trunks

The Trunks has got to be the craziest band I was ever in. It included three former members of Wally who had previously been signed to Atlantic records. Wally was something of a cross between Yes and Crosby, Stills and Nash, but times and the music had changed and they lost their recording contract. I'd supported them a couple of times at Harrogate's Royal Hall and at the Harrogate Theatre. They were a popular band and always packed out these venues.

Paul Middleton was Wally's lap-steel guitarist and he'd been a side man yet an essential part of their sound. He wanted to sing his own songs so the

The Trunks. L-R; CJ, Roger Harrison, Everton,
John Massey, Paul Middleton and Alex Crosby

two of us started rehearsing with guitarist Robbie Forester at Paul's house off Montpellier. We booked a gig at the notorious Wanderers Club, a cellar bar frequented by crooks, drunks, dope dealers and, generally, the dubious end of the social spectrum, so we fitted right in there. If the police were looking for anyone suspected of a felony, the Wanderers was the first place to look. That's probably the only reason they didn't close it down, despite relentless complaints from the more conservative population of Harrogate. Norman, the landlord, dealt with the nightly deluge of broken glass with a lawnmower which saved him sweeping up.

We didn't yet have a drummer or a bass player so Pete Cosker, Wally's guitarist, offered to play bass. We asked a friend called Jeff, who'd never played drums in his life, to play drums. Paul told him, "Just do this, bang thump, bang thump. That's right, just like that and keep going whatever happens." Robbie bottled out of the gig at the last minute and didn't tell us. He didn't turn up until we'd finished and I could have cheerfully throttled him.

We kicked off the first song and the energy level from Paul and I was frightening, fuelled by our anger at Robbie and our determination to blow the roof off the place. It worked and word soon got around. Wally's bass

The Trunks. L-R; CJ, Everton, Roger Harrison, Cliffy Lee, Frank Mizen, John Massey, Alex Crosby and, playing his ironing board, Paul Middleton

player Frank Mizen took over on bass and Pete went back to playing lead guitar.

We soon landed a residency at the Cock and Castle, another notorious Harrogate pub where Wally had started out. Paul's elder brother, Johnny, brought along his African drum. Cliffy Lee (stage name – Cornelius Hydrant) became our drummer and we soon became the talk of the town. A scene developed very quickly. Although the landlord broadcast the fact that he hated our band, he was happy to have us there regularly because we packed the place out and, consequently, he sold a lot of beer.

Paul wanted to call the band Flotsam and Jetsam. It was a good name and very appropriate, considering that our rock n' roll dreams had been bulldozed by the punk movement and we were generally feeling washed up. These were desperate days and Paul summed up our situation in his song, I'm only Human; 'Well, they're standing in a line, take a look at them broken wasted boys. They travelled too far, too fast through rock 'n' roll."

But Flotsam and Jetsam didn't stick and you'll probably recall those nights when you all sit around thinking of a band name; eventually the person who comes up with the stupidest name wins. In this case it was Frank who suggested The Trunks, which caused much hilarity. It had so many connotations. So, it was unanimous, The Trunks it was. Johnny Middleton, being a talented artist, immediately got busy designing posters. On one, he cut out the shape of an elephant from a magazine advertisement for a kitchenette.

Cliffy Lee, our drummer, was a dustbin man and he'd furnished his place lavishly with some choice pieces of furniture and Persian carpets, thrown out by the rich folks on Kent Road. He had a gambling addiction and the only time I've been in a bookies in my life was to retrieve Cliffy because we were late for a gig. On one memorable occasion he took the door money from a gig and put it on a horse and, of course, the inevitable happened. I went round to his flat, suspecting I had very little chance of retrieving the money, and walked into the living room where he was seated cross-legged on a Persian rug. I didn't need to ask. Cliffy Lee the gambler hung his head and looked at the floor, "It wor' a dead cert."

Before Cliffy joined, we'd had an Italian guy, Rosario, drum for us. He was very enthusiastic but there was one fatal flaw. Occasionally he would unknowingly switch and play the beat backwards. That's the only way I can explain it. Paul and I found it amusing and so went with it. If anything happened during a performance, we went with it anyway so what the hell.

It was Saturday lunchtime and I was telling my friend Mike Dalligan that The Trunks were booked for a gig that night and there was no PA available. "No problem," said Mike, who was a huge Trunks fan and used to problem solving. He was suddenly initiated into the unglamourous side of life in a rock 'n' roll band as we spent the entire day and covered many miles locating one. That evening, as we were about to go on stage, Pete Cosker announced that he didn't have a guitar because he was "so out of it, man." I dashed out, making numerous phone calls and finally managed to borrow one with minutes to spare.

How did I ever wind up being the sensible guy in this cowboy outfit? Inevitably, Pete left, though he was a fine guitarist no matter what bad shape he was in. He went the way of many acid casualties and he wasn't long for this world. It was sad to see a handsome young guy turn into a "park bench mutation" as Neil Young so eloquently put it.

The next version of The Trunks had Paul and I sharing the vocals, John Massey on guitar, Frank Mizen on bass, Alex Crosby on drums and Everton on congas. Eventually I managed to get Dodger and Richard in the band. There was a lot of charisma and a lot of talent in The Trunks, along with too many personal problems.

After a gig in York, we arrived back in Harrogate in the early hours and left our equipment at a friend's house, conveniently around the corner from the Wanderers. The next morning, I went to collect my gear and, where my Hammond organ had been, I was staring at a hole in space. I thought I knew who'd stolen it but I couldn't prove it. My dad was naturally concerned and came with me to the police station. The sergeant went into the office and came back with a long list of undesirables. The six names at the top of the list were the members of The Trunks. My name was second on the list after Paul's. There was clearly no intention of investigating the theft.

I made the tragic mistake of falling for Paul's younger brother's wife. I was sitting in the pub one afternoon, having a drink with the two of them when she asked him what he wanted for his tea. A simple question but it twisted deep inside me like a knife, like a sledgehammer to my heart. What wouldn't I do for her to say that to me?

Consequently, things went quickly downhill from there. In the summer I threw some wild parties at Park Lodge and inevitably, my world spiralled out of control. It seemed like everyone I knew and a whole bunch of people I didn't know started turning up. I soon learned to my cost that when a notorious rock'n'roll band becomes the scene, it can attract the wrong crowd very quickly. As bad luck would have it, Pete Coraine arrived at my house; he was a huge guy and I hardly knew him, but he announced that he had five hundred tabs of acid and a black belt in karate. Could he hide out for a few days? An offer I was in no position to refuse.

Inevitably the drug squad arrived at Park Lodge. Pete Coraine had moved on by then and when the squad cars arrived, I met them at the gate, invited them in and asked them if they would like a cup of tea. My one concern was the dope plant I'd grown from seed in the back garden but they weren't interested, they had much bigger fish to fry. Nevertheless, their visit would soon have repercussions.

A few weeks before, a good friend at the time, had arrived on the doorstep with his wife and small child. John was a wild boy and completely irresponsible. Still, he was lots of fun and they were homeless so I invited them to stay. They'd been there for several weeks and didn't seem in any hurry to leave any time soon. Then when he tried to pass a forged banknote at the Fford Green in Leeds, John gave Park Lodge, Ripley as his address. Imagine Lady Ingleby at a coffee morning, opening the Harrogate Herald and her friend pointing out that a man had been arrested and had given the address of one of her sitting tenants.

Unsurprisingly, I got my eviction notice a few days later.

79

So You Wanna Be a Rock 'n' Roll Star

Paul Buckley told me this story; he was playing a gig and as he'd written a new song, he thought he'd try it out. There were only eight people in the small pub including the two guys at the bar. The new song was going very well, so well in fact that by the time he was getting to the final chorus, he was feeling very pleased and was starting to congratulate himself on such a stunning first performance. The song finished. Nothing. Deafening silence.

A few seconds went by, then one of the guys at the bar turned to the other, "I see Burnley won again."

80

Exiles Intact

Chapeltown had once been the Jewish ghetto; the big houses on Spencer Place had belonged to doctors and solicitors. When my mother was a girl, her first job on leaving school was with a Jewish tailor, known as Pappa Eudall. His factory was opposite the old synagogue, which is now the Northern Dance Centre on Chapeltown Road. When the Jewish community became more affluent, they moved further out of Leeds to Moortown and in the fifties and sixties, the Caribbean community, the Windrush generation moved in. It's been the West Indian ghetto ever since.

I moved to Chapeltown in the mid-seventies where there was a thriving music scene. House parties, formerly known as shebeens, were renamed "blues." Blues were usually held in dark cellars, installed with huge sound systems, the black youths jostling for position at the microphone, rapping over dub reggae rhythms with the emphasis on deep bass and drums. With a strong smell of ganga permeating the proceedings, the older men could be found in the back room usually playing cards or dominoes and always someone selling cans of Red Stripe at highly exorbitant prices.

By the time I lived in Chapeltown, Spencer Place had become the red-light district. Early mornings, returning home from a blues on a winter's night, the working girls would be standing there freezing their asses off but they'd always say hi. By now I was a local and they knew I wasn't a potential punter. Some of them were just trying to feed their families and would turn a trick just to be able to buy groceries. It was a dangerous occupation, particularly at that time when the Yorkshire Ripper was targeting young women and several of his victims were found murdered in the Chapeltown area. It was dangerous for any woman walking alone in Chapeltown after dark. Women visitors had to be chaperoned and many nights I walked women friends to their front doors.

Dodger and Richard joined Wolfrace, the big reggae band in Chapeltown, in 1979. They were backing Laurel Aitkin, an old guy from Jamaica at the International Club. He'd had a big hit with Neil Diamond's Red Red Wine. I was talking to Aitkin in the dressing room before they went on stage; he told me, "Bob Marley 'be nothing without me." I took this for bragging but later I found out there was some truth in what he said. Those old guys had been early pioneers of Ska and Blue-Beat.

As Keith Richard pointed out recently, "Rock music is a white version of rock n'roll, all rock and no roll. They turn it into a march." He was lucky enough to be living in Jamaica for a time and he moved there for good reason. Reggae was a relatively new music and not unlike the early days of rock n'roll, it was an exciting time to be around. It had great grooves and was giving young black people a new sense of identity. I'd venture to say that spiritually, Bob Marley brought his people out of the wilderness, another Brother Moses.

Following the Toxteth riots in Liverpool in 1981, that July there were riots in Chapeltown. Racial tensions were ignited by a combination of inner-city poverty, poor housing and unemployment.

Dodger was looking out of his front window on Cowper Street, when he witnessed an extremely violent collision between police and rioters, on the corner right outside his front door. A gang of angry rioters arrived from Toxteth intent on burning and looting. Local guys surrounded their car repair shop to stop them dragging the cars out and torching them. They also stood guard to protect their local grocery, Warsaw Stores. I walked down Chapeltown Road the morning after the riots and the petrol station had been torched. Shop windows were smashed but Warsaw Stores had survived. The proprietor was in tears but grateful to the local youths that she was still in business.

In the early eighties, Dodger and I joined the next important reggae band from those same Chapeltown streets, Exiles Intact. It was formed around two sisters, Paulette and Annette Morris. Their father, St Clair Morris, ran the Paradise Steel Band and a lot of local musicians learned music coming up through that band and through the gospel church. Like many of the local Caribbean population, Paulette and Annette's family were originally from Saint Kitts. The sisters were, and still are brilliant singers and in recent years they've sung on my albums. When I first met them, they were young, straight from church, competing in what was very much a man's world. Paulette in particular was strong and determined to get their original songs heard.

Annette's partner, Carl, was the drummer and Danman, the rhythm guitarist. The four of them had known each other some time, and would sit in a room, amid heated debate, eventually coming out with a song. I was intrigued to find out how this worked, so one day, I sat in the corner, kept quiet and watched. They would argue about lyrics saying, "You can't say that, it's not realistic."

If, for example, Berry Gordy had come along in those days to start a record company like Motown, he need have looked no further for the real stars. Carl would have been the next Michael Jackson with his singing and drumming skills and his good looks. Paulette and her sister would have been the Martha and the Vandellas and, in fact, they did become the Vandellas years later when they toured this country with Martha Reeves.

Dodger played lead guitar, Steve Skellington played bass, and I played Hammond organ. I didn't sing in this band, there was no need, and I never even mentioned to them that I could sing. Roman was a young Polish guy with a black Beatle haircut who played synthesizer. He always dressed in black so we called him Roman Black, (as in rum 'n' black). Roman Remains was his other nick-name. We played the Trades Club in Chapeltown and we stood on stage behind our instruments for a good twenty minutes, in front of a full house, waiting impatiently for Danman, who was late. It turned out that all that time, he was still having his hair processed. When he did finally show, tempers were frayed and angry words exchanged although, I have to say, his hair did look quite spectacular.

There was a reggae festival at the Queen's Hall with some top bands booked including Yellowman. Unfortunately, the promoters had failed to

Annette and Paulette Morris

201

mention that they hadn't budgeted any money to pay the bands. Consequently, things got rather heated backstage and when guns appeared, I decided to take my leave and slipped into the audience. Maxi Priest explained the situation to the crowd; as he wasn't getting paid, he would perform one song for the audience, which he did as a gesture of good will. We had performed our set long before the trouble started and I, for one, was just glad to get out of there in one piece.

81

Enufsed

When Everton, the Trunks' conga player, was six years old, he spent his final day in the Caribbean on a beach under clear blue skies with two friends, climbing a palm tree and leaping off it into the sea. The next day, with his family, he boarded a plane to England. It was the middle of winter, freezing cold and raining when they arrived at what is now Leeds and Bradford airport. His aunty met them off the plane and presented him with a balaclava she'd knitted to keep his head warm. Then they were driven to her house and he sat in a room in front of a one bar electric fire, feeling like he'd just come from heaven and arrived in the bowels of hell itself.

Everton found us a cellar off North Street which became our rehearsal room. Some of these bands overlapped. I'd be in the Trunks and Exiles Intact, at the same time, occasionally playing with the King Bees. When The Trunks or Exiles weren't using the rehearsal room, other bands used it. One of these bands was Enufsed, recently formed by the Shand brothers who, I later found out, grew up on Rosebank Grove, the same street of back-to-backs in Leeds where I'd first lived as a small boy.

Paul and Peter Shand were both well over six feet tall, good-looking, Asian- Caribbean guys in their mid-twenties. They'd had a difficult upbringing and consequently they'd had to become tough. They had muscles like iron and had cultivated something of a reputation. Dodger would open up the cellar for them so he started sitting in on their sessions. He told me how good they were and as my Hammond was already set up down there, I went and sat in too. They were funky as hell.

Peter Shand's bass playing was frightening, every bit as intimidating as his persona. He was still in the Airforce at the time (he was the man who sprayed those Red Arrows aeroplanes red) and he would arrive on Friday evening in full uniform all geared up and ready to put the unk back in the funk. We had to snap to attention and be there on time, after all, there was no way we would want to upset him. Although when you got to know him, he was a pussycat. Eventually he left the Airforce and became a lot more chilled once the pressure was off. Peter's elder brother Paul played rhythm guitar. His right hand was like lightning, a karate-chop style so slick it made the music pop and fizz.

Tony Tyrrell looked like a young Curtis Mayfield, wore glasses, played synthesizer and had a great feel for the funk. He wasn't a technical player but he knew how to add atmosphere and sweetness to the groove. Charley Hutchinson was a cool steady drummer, nothing flash. Dodger and I fit right in there; Dodger became lead guitarist and I became their organist and lead singer. We soon became obsessed with this music and when Paul left the Airforce, we played just about every afternoon. That's when we moved to another studio in Chapeltown belonging to the Professor. The Professor had built the studio in his cellar with a window into a separate control room. The only problem was he couldn't yet afford the recording equipment so, in the meantime, he let us use it as our rehearsal room.

Dodger and I were the two Spooks in the band, the white guys. The black guys often referred to each other using the N' word. Because we would never use that word, Dodger and I would refer to each other as Honky.

The Shand brothers had nick-names for everyone. They called Charley 'Trillions of Teeth', Dodger became Rupert because he's a natural leader so they named him after Rupert the Bear. He'd argue, "I'm not just a friendly little bear you know." They named me Eddie because I have a large head, hat-size seven and a quarter. They referred to Tony as 'Icca Boy wi' Glasses.'

Our first gig was at Coconut Grove, a nightclub in the Grand Arcade. I was surprised to realise that despite their musical expertise, the Shands had never gigged before. We were playing up on a balcony and these two hard men were crouching down, hiding in the shadows. That didn't last long. At the next gig, as soon as they got the audience's attention, they were up on their feet striding around at the front of the stage like bronze adonises.

Not a word that one would normally expect to hear in a band rehearsal room but for some reason the word 'crouton' came up in conversation. The Shands looked at each other and fell about laughing. It transpired that, when they were teenagers and were caught on the train without a ticket, they would pretend to be foreigners, inventing their very own African language. When challenged, they would look puzzled and enquire, 'Crouton?' They would look concerned, turn to each other and one would ask, 'Mabooto matumba?' The other would reply something like 'Abooto wah wah matumba?' They would then turn to the poor ticket man, with wide eyed innocence and ask again, 'Crouton?'

We played the Trades Club in Chapeltown, supporting The Steve Gibbons Band. It was for the Blue Angels, the Leeds chapter of the Hell's Angels. Enufsed had been playing so regularly that we could anticipate each other musically. If inspired, people took chances; at one point, Dodger drove the song right off a cliff and miraculously we caught him. Our sound man, Howard Richards, would turn up the echo, dub-reggae style, at the end of a song. He was a master of the art of adding reverb and echo. The Steve Gibbons Band were watching us from the wings and were full of enthusiasm when we came off stage. Then I was grabbed by a pretty female Hell's Angel who asked me to dance. I'd been dancing for only a few minutes when I happened to turn around. The Shand Brothers were collapsed on the floor laughing while Tony Tyrrell was lying sideways across two bar-stools holding his stomach. At the next rehearsal, Paul Shand did an impression of me dancing saying, "This is Chris walking on to the dance-floor," to much hilarity. I have to tell you I have never danced since. It's common knowledge that men have to be either gay or black, preferably both, in order to dance. Straight white guys tend to dance like Prince Charles, with few exceptions to the rule.

Years later, I was watching a band and the young West Indian drummer came over and told me he'd seen me when he was a kid, with Enufsed at the Trades Club. He said it was his first gig. You never forget your first gig and he told me it inspired him to take up the drums, which made my day.

Dodgy dealings – CJ and Paul Shand

One afternoon, Charley and I were down in the rehearsal room. We had Frankie Beverly and Maze blasting out over the PA and Charley started singing along. I don't believe Charley had any idea he had such a great voice and I was amazed. I called a band meeting right away and we all stood in a circle. I told them I'd heard Charley sing and proposed that we make him the lead singer. I explained that I was happy to sing back-up. I liked singing harmony and, anyway, the band needed a black singer. Howard Richards stepped forward. He told me, "I know Charley better than you and if you do this, Chris, I guarantee, it will break up the band."

He was right.

In the mean-time we played a gig at a big disco in Leeds city centre and just about the whole of Chapeltown turned out to see us. Charley was now the new front-man so we'd recruited Keith Jackson on drums. He was given the nickname Keef the Chief as he looked like a young tribal chief, charismatic with long dreadlocks down over his shoulders. Keith got more house than anyone when it came to band introductions.

I met Keith years later. He'd cut his hair short and was drumming with Stomp, performing in theatres worldwide. I mentioned that he'd hardly said a word when he was in Enufsed. He said that was because he was so in awe of everyone. I told him, "Keith, we were in awe of you."

The Shand brothers were now acting like kings when they hit that stage and I was glad to see them being recognised for their talent, if only by their local community. They were bad boys but like a lot of bad guys, they were great fun. Inevitably I suppose, I heard Paul wound up in prison. The last I heard, Peter was in America and playing in the New Mastersounds. I heard he'd been jamming with the Meters and playing just the kind of funk he always loved.

82

The Great Todmorden Flood

I borrowed my wife's car. The plan was to drive over to Johnny Vincent's house, load my gear into his car and travel to the duo gig together. It was Johnny who suggested that, as he only had his amp and a couple of guitars, it would be easier to drive to Todmorden in Jane's car. As we drove down the Calder Valley, we noticed heavy black clouds appearing over the Pennine hills, like some dreadful omen.

The pub was called The House That Jack Built and we could immediately see why. The floor of the bar was on a substantial slope. The landlord indicated the performance area at the lower end. We parked the car outside the pub and, as we unloaded our equipment, a light rain began to fall, which rapidly became heavier as we started the first set. We were encouraged by the lively (if already well-lubricated) audience.

Halfway through our first set I looked out of the window and observed a river beginning to flow along the road. I noticed with mounting anxiety that the pub door was considerably lower than the street and by the time we started our second set the river was turning into a raging torrent. I looked down and was slightly bewildered to see my plug board was floating. Suddenly the door burst open and we watched a small tsunami plunge towards us at the deep end. First reaction; switch off the power, grab foot pedals, guitars, anything, grab amps, keyboards, lift them onto tables, windowsills, anywhere above the water, which was suddenly up to our knees and rising.

Across the bar were some stairs, presumably leading to a room where we might store our gear in safety (assuming the building didn't wash away entirely in the flood.) By the time we were carrying the last of our gear upstairs, water was up to my waist. We had to wade even further down the sloping floor into the cold water to reach the stairs. Thoughts of Wallace Hartley, the band leader on the Titanic, came to mind.

It was then that the landlord made the crucially catastrophic decision to announce free beer for all. Clearly the beer barrels were already submerged in river water and the beer would otherwise be wasted so he thought he would make the most of the opportunity to ingratiate himself with the locals. Naturally this proved popular and customers were now happily refilling their glasses, standing waist deep in dirty water which had been forced up through the drains; they wouldn't let a little sewage dampen their spirits. They were determined to take advantage of his generous offer. It was closing time but the celebrations, if you could call them that, would continue late into the night, at least until the beer ran out. Everyone in the pub was trapped until the water subsided anyway, whenever that might be.

We stored our gear on several old church pews. I looked out of the upstairs window at a fast-flowing, turbulent flood of mud and detritus. There was little sign of my wife's car, just the top of the roof poking out of the floodwaters.

The locals were getting rowdy by now and inevitably a fight broke out. Two strapping local lasses were soon brawling, pushing each other until they both fell over in the water. It was like a scene from a western with the crowd cheering them on. This was the Yorkshire equivalent of the Appalachian Mountains. There was thrashing and screaming and pulling of hair until the poor landlord finally decided to call time. It was another hour before the waters subsided sufficiently and he managed to evict the last drunken cus-

tomer, threatening and cursing.

I was listening to all this propped upright, seated on a hard church pew upstairs between two PA speakers. Johnny was seated opposite me on another pew, with his head resting on a guitar case and I was just beginning to fall asleep when he started to snore. He snored continuously and loudly for the next few hours until daylight when, not having had any sleep at all, I made my way to the window and looked out at a sea of mud and destruction. Thankfully the waters had subsided and luckily Jane's car was still there, though who knew what state it would be in.

With some degree of trepidation, I eventually opened the driver's door. Water gushed out and it stank of sewage. It was hardly worth even trying to start it. No internal combustion engine could have survived such an ordeal. Nevertheless, despite approximately twelve hours of immersion in diluted sewage, I tried the ignition and almost miraculously, the engine coughed, choked and spluttered into life. We wiped the seats as well as we could with paper towels and loaded the car. I remember we didn't have the heart to ask the landlord to pay us under the circumstances.

Driving back along the Calder Valley, it looked like a war zone. We had to navigate and weave our way past broken trees, torn up fences, earth piled up like snowdrifts, stones thrown everywhere from dry-stone walls, piles of detritus and even a bewildered cow standing in the middle of the road.

The thing that worried me the most was the thought of having to explain all this to my wife. The valeting bill would be quite substantial and I would have to promise only ever to use my own car in any future ventures.

"Move over little dog 'cos the big dog's movin' in". 1

Hank Williams

83

The Juke Boys

It was the height of the troubles in Northern Ireland and at our regular Wednesday night residency at the Harrogate Blues Bar, the Juke Boys were playing the rock classic, Riot in Cell Block Number Nine.[1] This particular night, Dougie Brister decided he was going to perform it in an Ian Paisley accent; "Thurs a roiat goin' orn." He could easily have caused a riot himself but luckily it went down a storm.

I'd given up smoking when my youngest daughter, Zana, was born, although for some years, I still smoked the occasional funny cigarette. (These days I've curbed all those excesses.) Like most tobacco addicts, I found it difficult to quit and would position myself downwind of many a smoking acquaintance. I reckon it took me about six months before I'd stopped noticing people lighting up and focusing on lit cigarette ends in the audience. Returning home from a gig at the Blues Bar, my daughter Emily asked me to go and change my clothes because she said I smelt of smoke; I hadn't noticed, and that's when I realised, I'd quit. Since the smoking ban there is one thing I miss; when I open the cupboard where I keep my musical equipment, it's not the same. It doesn't smell of rock n' roll any more.

One night during the interval, Buck Mosey, the Juke Boys' drummer, said his American cousin, a brilliant drummer, was in town. He asked if we'd mind if Dwain sat in with us. Just before the second set, Dwain came over and introduced himself; he had a mass of black hair, a huge beard, a strong southern American accent and was wearing a shirt which looked like it had been made from a Confederate flag. He shook my hand and promptly took his place behind the drums. We kicked off the first number and Dwain's style of drumming seemed very familiar. His drumming was very much like Buck's. In fact, it was exactly like Bucks' and then the penny dropped.

Dougie and Gwynn Jones, the bass player, both had remote transmitters on their guitars so they didn't need guitar leads, meaning they could go walk about through the crowd, still playing while chatting to people, sometimes venturing as far as the bar upstairs. On one occasion they were gone for a considerable time while Buck and I continued to play, wondering where they'd disappeared; it was a freezing winter night, snowing a blizzard - surely, they hadn't gone outside into the street? Bands at The Blues Bar play with their backs to the window, so we couldn't see what was happening. The group van was parked directly across the pavement in full view of the audience and suddenly there was a massive cheer from the crowded bar. Soon everyone was on their feet laughing and pointing. Buck and I turned around; miraculously, without missing a note, the two of them had managed to climb onto the van roof in the ice and snow and with legs astride, were momentarily transformed into the Rock Gods they were always meant to be.

84

Band Politics

Johnny Vincent was talking to his band leader, when the drummer came over and started to complain about the bass player. He said, "He's holding us back." The band leader replied, "Why, where are we going?"

85

Frank
(The Blues Doctors)

I was walking through the supermarket with Frank Mizen and Kung Fu Fighting [1] was playing.

"I played on this," said Frank."
"You played on Kung Fu Fighting?"
"Yeh, me and Steve Ferrone."
"You mean Steve Ferrone who played drums for the Average White Band and now plays for Tom Petty and the Heartbreakers?"
"Yeh, me and Steve Ferrone."

Back in the early seventies, Frank Mizen was in a band called Gomez who were recording demos at EMI, hopefully with a chance of a recording contract. EMI asked Gomez' lead singer, Carl Douglas, to consider recording one of his songs which they thought would be a sure-fire hit. Carl brought the song along to the band and they laughed him out of the room. Steve Ferrone, who was the drummer in Gomez, collared Frank who was the trombonist; as they were both skint, Ferrone suggested that the two of them do the session as he knew Frank also played bass. Frank agreed and they had the choice of either taking a royalty payment or the fifteen quid session fee. They took the session fee because the song was crap and was never going to be a hit.

Kung Fu Fighting sold millions and is still played worldwide.

Frank started out playing trombone in the National Youth Orchestra. He reckoned the trombone players in an orchestra are usually the piss heads and you could guarantee to find them later down the pub. As a teenager, Frank won a scholarship to study on the conductor's course at the Royal College of Music. When he left college, he did a tour playing trombone with the Jackson Five. Many years later we were in a soul band, together with a four-piece brass section, called The Blues Doctors, which Frank liked to refer to as the Blues Dentists.

The two of us were seated at the piano writing brass parts for a song of mine. I'd sing my idea for the main brass line and Frank would write down the tune in notation. I was amazed to discover he could write down the notes just about as fast as I could sing them. Then he'd make any improvements he thought the tune needed and fill in the other harmony brass parts. After studying Wagner and Beethoven scores this was no difficulty for him at all.

Queen was recording demos at EMI, just down the corridor, at the same time as Gomez. Frank and Roger Taylor had been doing session work together as they were both skint. Roger called by one day to see if Frank could put some bass on a song Queen was recording and Frank agreed. He'd walked past their open door a couple of times and heard what they were doing and played the bass part with no rehearsal, first take. Roger returned some minutes later to say that Freddie and Brian really liked his bass part and asked if Frank could record some more as they didn't have a bass player; they were effectively offering him the job. Frank said he'd help them out, but was committed to Gomez.

Frank Mizen with feline friend at the controls

Years later Frank was playing trombone in Zoot and the Roots, who were supporting Roger's band, The Cross. At the sound check, Roger tapped him on the shoulder, "I didn't know you played trombone, Frank, I thought you were a bass player."

I'd known Frank forty years before he told me these stories.

The Old Bourbon was the Cajun restaurant across the road from Harrogate's Royal Hall, where, if you remember, we'd finished off the night when The Blues Doctors supported The Pretty Things.

Richard Fox, who had originally started The Blues Bar, eventually realised his dream to have a restaurant and an adjoining venue with some big names appearing as well as supporting local talent. To this end he employed four of us to play his restaurant, each taking it in turns on a rota system. So, for Rob Reynolds, Jason Feddy, Gwyn Jones and myself, playing every fourth night, it was the nearest any of us got to a steady job.

Gwyn and I played piano but I found I didn't have the strength in my hands to pound that big grand piano for hours. Gwyn had no problem but I would bring my electric piano and set it up in front of the grand piano.

It was the first time I'd played solo since the University tour in '74. I was playing New Orleans classics as well as blues and boogie woogie. It was a lovely atmosphere, the walls painted in scenes from New Orleans, tables with mis- matched chairs, the smell of Cajun food and ground coffee, lots of interesting people, pretty women, friends dropping by. I felt at home there.

One night my future wife walked in and we've been together ever since.

The Old Bourbon served coffee in the traditional American way; free top-up all night long served from a coffee machine the size of a Ford Cortina bolted to the wall. My wife always maintained you didn't need alcohol for a high when you had their coffee – it kept you buzzing all night. Years later she asked the chef, Nick, what type of coffee it was, and was surprised when he told her a mundane, easily available supermarket brand. After some thought he said, "Mind you, I put anything into that machine I happened to have in my pocket; dope mostly, but I remember bunging in a couple of tabs of acid on several occasions."

I was playing the piano and must've had my eyes closed because when I opened them, the entire Jools Holland Orchestra was sitting in front of me.

I'd opened my eyes because I could hear someone was joining in on the grand piano behind me and when I turned around it was Jools.

He'd recently hosted a programme about boogie woogie, so I asked him to show me a couple of left-hand boogie patterns which I still use to this day.

On another occasion I was playing Fats Domino's Blueberry Hill, when from the dancehall next door, I heard the distant sound of the riff played on the saxophone. The riff grew gradually louder and as Chris (Snake) Davis appeared in the doorway, the place erupted. The restaurant was packed with punters, having a drink or a meal before seeing the Snake Davis Band later that night. Chris joined me on stage, staying there for the rest of the set. Some years earlier, we'd played together in a five-piece band with Keith Jeavons, Johnny White and Johnny Vincent. We had a residency at the Harrogate Arms and sometimes, Chris would turn up late because he'd been teaching. Whenever he did arrive, everyone's playing automatically went up a notch, he's that good. I played a Hammond L100 in those days through a massive Lesley cabinet the size of a small wardrobe. At the end of the night, when the other guys waltzed off with young women (sax players being particularly popular in that department) I'd look at the drummer and say, "Why did we chose these instruments?" I have to say Chris was a gentleman and he'd always stay behind and help me carry my gear to the car, navigating up and down fire escapes often covered in ice on winter's nights.

Next time, if there is a next time, I'm taking up the saxophone.

Jon Martyn appeared at the Old Bourbon and we were pleased to connect with each other again. He was on fine form, playing his Gibson SG with a mesmerising echo effect. Years later I saw him perform one of his last gigs just before he died. He slurred his words so much by this time, you couldn't tell what he was singing about unless you knew the song but his voice, his tone was deep and rich, just beautiful.

I'd just completed my set in the restaurant, playing the Professor Longhair New Orleans classic, Big Chief. I went through to the venue next door, to see Jon Cleary sound checking for his solo performance that night. I'd never heard of him but straight away he seemed like one hell of a piano player, so I asked him if he knew Big Chief. He looked at me sideways with a look that said, you have no idea what's about to come your way. Suddenly the guy had six pairs of hands. It went past me so fast I was in shock.

That night his performance was staggering, not just his piano playing but his singing and his song writing. I locked myself in my room for three days, seriously considering a career in accountancy.

A few weeks later I went to see him at the Duchess in Leeds and there were only fifteen people in the place so I met him at the bar and bought him a drink. I asked him what was next on his agenda and he told me he was playing on a Taj Mahal album along with Eric Clapton. That was Senior Blues and he went on to play with Bonnie Raitt, soon becoming the to go-to piano player. He only has to play a couple of notes and you can tell it's him. So now I didn't feel so bad, knowing he's the best in the world. Let's put it this way, at Doctor John's birthday bash, Jon Cleary played the piano and the good Doctor played guitar.

The Blues Doctors were formed around the Old Bourbon and we became a regular feature. We were a Blues-Brothers-type outfit with Rob Donnelly as the short fat front man and me as the tall skinny one. Rob was lead guitarist and I played keyboards. Rob has a high tenor voice which contrasted well with my baritone. What always interests me is seeing a band full of real characters and in this band, there was no shortage of novelty personalities. The brass section alone had enough charisma between them, and you couldn't easily take your eyes off them; there was Frank on trombone, looking like he was on loan from ZZ Top, Grant Kirkup on trumpet, dark and handsome, at the microphone, between songs, affectionately, and yet mercilessly taking the piss out of our fat front-man. Big Dave from Scarborough was on tenor sax, a bear of a man, and pint-sized Wayne Robinson on alto sax, when he was back from three-week stints, working on an oil-rig in the North Sea. We had the Juke Boys Rhythm section, Gwyn Jones on bass and Buck Mosey on drums. Ashley Reeks eventually took over on bass; eccentric is an understatement; a multi-talented musician and comedian who has been known to per-

"Frank, get your axe!"

form forward rolls while playing the bass, a veritable Tommy Cooper and a thoroughly nice guy.

Ashley was once on tour in America with Frank Dunnery. They were travelling through the deep-south and the two of them pulled into a gas station to fill up. The proprietor, who was clearly on a tooth-share scheme, looked at them with one funny eye and said, "You strangers round here, aint yer boys? They don't like strangers round here. Last strangers round here got gang banged."

One night I was having a late drink with Wayne after a gig at the Old Bourbon. It was after midnight and he told me what he'd be doing later that morning; Buck was going to drive him to Hull where he'd be taken to the oil-rig for a fire- drill. It was the middle of winter and he would be pushed off the edge of the rig in a rubber dinghy into the freezing North Sea. Maybe he thought it would take the edge off it if he had a hangover. Wayne worked as a rig diver; he went for life insurance and was told the only job considered more dangerous than his was lion-tamer.

Wayne would be home for one week in four. The rest of the brass section joined the Little Angels and went on American stadium tours supporting Brian Adams, ZZ Top and Eddie Van Halen. Grant is an amazing rock guitarist as well as a fine trumpet player and at the end of the tour Van Halen gave him one of his signature guitars.

One evening, following a successful gig, a club owner decided he couldn't afford to pay us. Rob Donnelly took charge; he comes from a large Irish family. If you knock down one Donnelly, there's another one standing right behind him. He turned to Frank Mizen, who had just had an unusually severe haircut, and said loudly, "Frank, get your axe." Frank went out to his car and returned, standing in silhouette in the open doorway, in the light of a full moon brandishing his felling axe.

We got paid.

We played a gig in Darlington; there was a row of pin-ball machines at the back of the room, and as we played our first set most of the audience was ignoring us, more interested in the machines. Eventually I just lost it and, with the band going full-tilt started yelling insults at the audience. The whole thing was being recorded on tape, played back later to much hilarity. Eventually I did manage to clear the place and Frank told me I could have been in serious trouble had someone decided to take a swing at me. He was right of course but when you see red, you don't always consider the consequences. There was a black guy sitting at the front who thought the whole thing was hilarious.

Surprisingly, we were booked back. I thought the best thing I could do was go in disguise. Rob was driving and I was in the passenger seat wearing a bushy red false beard, a trilby and a big overcoat. The rest of The Blues Doctors were in the van and as they overtook us, they were wondering who the old guy was.

The first set went well and this time there was a much bigger audience. I apologised profusely for the appalling behaviour of our previous keyboard player and thanked the management for booking us back, after all it was very big of them considering. The same guy who'd enjoyed my incendiary tirade the last time was back again sitting at the front. He obviously didn't cotton on until I leaned forward and pulled down the false beard, revealing my true identity, (this was well before Oh Brother Where Art Thou). He almost fell off his chair.

The Blues Doctors. L-R; Back Row – Wayne Robinson, Gwyn Jones, Frank Mizen, Buck Mosey. Front Row – Grant Kirkup, CJ, Rob Donnelly

219

86

Cat o' Nine Tails

Rob and Ashley are boxing enthusiasts. They spent a pleasant evening in the pub with an old guy they'd never met before. He seemed to be an authority on boxing and, leafing through the boxing books in Smith's stationers on Parliament Street, they were surprised to find the old man's photograph. It was obviously the same guy back in his youth. He was pictured training at the same London gym as the Kray twins. Eric Mason had grown up with the Krays. A hard East End gangster, it was reputed that he once wound up in hospital with an axe in his head. He had been attacked by Mad Frankie Frazer. The axe, from which he'd tried to defend himself, had sliced through his hand, pinning it to his head. He was in his mid-seventies when Rob and Ashley inadvertently made his acquaintance. Realising the notoriety of their new friend did not deter them in the least, but only fascinated them further.

Eric had been the last man in Britain to receive the Cat o' Nine Tails after attacking four prison officers. He was going to be featured in a television programme and was looking for a venue in Harrogate where he could invite his underworld friends on the night of the broadcast. Ashley and Rob immediately suggested The Old Bourbon. They also jumped at the opportunity to persuade him to book The Blues Doctors.

I arrived at the gig. Eric was standing next to a large television set holding court. Standing in a circle around the room, were some of the toughest characters you could ever imagine; some were mean-looking men Eric's age, some young, hard men. Standing with his back to me directly opposite Eric, was a guy in his late twenties, approximately six foot six, wide shoulders packed into a beautifully tailored black suit. His long black pony-tail reached right down to his ass, fists like hams.

I didn't hang about. I set up my equipment and soon the place was rammed.

The Blues Doctors kicked off the first set with the Peter Gunn theme, giving the brass section the spotlight. We played like our lives depended on it and that night we rocked the place. Coming off stage Rob motioned me over to the bar where I followed him cautiously as he pushed through the menacing crowd surrounding Eric. Standing at the bar, Eric now had the undivided attention of the bar-staff and was ordering drinks, passing them back to his buddies. Unabashed, Rob tapped his new pal on the shoulder and introduced me, up close and personal. I looked him in the eye and, though I was looking at an old man, the look he gave me was terrifying. I tried to keep my cool and hold it together. No one had ever looked at me like that and I'll be glad if I never see that look again. I needed a stiff drink.

The Godfather stood by the TV set as his underworld friends resumed their positions in the circle surrounding him. A reverential silence ensued as the programme played. There was much celebration afterwards as The Blues Doctors played on into the early hours. There was no question of finishing until the man said so.

87

The Lime Kilns

My family lived in a village between Harrogate and Ripon. The lime kilns were in the old quarry on the edge of the village and they were my personal Laurel Canyon. If you are at all familiar with the John Mayall record, you will understand. It was a place where I could go alone and sit quietly enjoying the nature around me. On warm summer days when my kids were small, we'd go for walks down there and then spend glorious afternoons paddling in the stream at the bottom of the lane. We have lots of happy memories of the place.

One day when my daughter, Zana, was four or five, we were walking down the lane heading for the lime kilns when I noticed a lone figure in the distance. As he walked up the hill towards us, I saw he was a middle-aged man dressed in a pair of shorts and a T-shirt, He was suntanned with long greying hair tied back in a ponytail. It was only when he had walked past us that I suddenly realised it was the man himself, John Mayall.

It would seem unlikely yet I'd heard rumours that he'd been seen in the village. It turned out that his sister lived nearby, and I realised I knew her. On reflection there was, indeed, a strong family resemblance. Returning from our walk, Zana and I made our way across the village green to the house where John Mayall's sister lived and, sure enough, the great man was sitting in the bay window. He answered the door and invited us in. I explained that I was a musician and that his music had a big influence on me and my fellow musicians, particularly in our teens. I recalled the story about seeing The Bluesbreakers with Eric Clapton, and going to the Marquee Club to see them when Keith Hartley and Mick Taylor were in his band.

When I was a student at Ealing, Eva Borganski was on my course; late one afternoon she announced that she had to leave because she was going to make tea for The Bluesbreakers. I went with her to see them at the Marquee and we got in early as she was "with the band". I remember Mayall sang The Death of J.B.Lenoir; it was a spellbinding rendition, about his friend who'd died in a car crash, performed solo on his nine-string guitar. Mick Taylor played brilliantly that night and I remember making a mental note of his clothes, he was about my build, thinking they would suit me. Later when he joined the Stones, for some reason, his dress sense seemed to go right out of the window.

Mayall asked me where I was playing so I told him we were playing the Blues Bar in Harrogate in a week's time. He said he was playing the Harrogate Conference Centre that same night with Peter Green and Mick Taylor and that if he got a chance, he'd try to get along to the Blues Bar. When I arrived home, I rang Johnny Vincent, "You'll never guess who I've been talking to." Johnny drove over immediately and that evening we called again to see Mayall. I introduced him to Johnny and we asked if he wanted to join us in the pub but he was having a meal with his family and we didn't want to intrude further. We talked for a few minutes, said we hoped to see him at the Blues Bar and said our farewells.

Arriving at the Blues Bar, Johnny produced several guitars and placed them carefully in a line on stands. He explained, "That one's for John Mayall, that one's for Peter Green, that one's for Mick Taylor and that one's for me." We tried to be realistic, but couldn't help constantly glancing at the door every time it opened. Sadly, our heroes didn't show that night and the much-anticipated superstar blues jam was destined to remain a beautiful dream. Thanks to Mayall's sister, Caroline, though, I do now have my signed copy of Laurel Canyon.

88

The King Ivory Band

Richard McFarlane and Chris Broughton put on local gigs, calling themselves The Booze Brothers. I'd known Chris since Art School days and he'd designed brilliant posters for the King Bees. Richard's friend Kevin Thorpe came from Retford and his band, Out of the Blue, were seriously good and regularly booked to play in Otley. (I love the name of Kevin's previous band – Norbert Trouble.)

Kevin heard the King Ivory Band and liked my songs. He'd recently had a studio room built onto his house in Retford and suggested I go down there for a couple of days and record some demos with him. Those two days were

The King Ivory Band. L-R; Johnny Vincent, Bob Duesbury, CJ, Bill White and Ian Rose

productive and turned out fortuitous for me. I'd recently met my future wife, Jane, and gave her a copy of the demos. She encouraged me to do something more with them.

Johnny Vincent and I had formed the King Ivory Band in 1995 with Bob Duesbury on bass, Bill White on Drums and Phil Snell on violin and mandolin. We took the band name from the nick-name Duffy gave me back in '71.

With this line-up we recorded the first proper album of my original songs, which was only available on cassette at first. Frank Mizen produced and engineered the album at Blue Strike studios in Harrogate and he did a fine job. Eventually Phil Snell left and Bill's friend Ian Rose joined on Hammond Organ. We subsequently recorded three albums

Tony Ridealgh's photograph for the front cover of The King Ivory Band's first album, L-R; CJ, Bob Duesbury, Bill White, Johnny Vincent and Phil Snell

Like Spinal Tap, the King Ivory Band went through a selection of drummers. Some might have spontaneously combusted, others had bizarre gardening accidents, but Rob Hirens moved to France. Rob's long, heavy curtains of hair obscured his face and would fly in all directions once he got into his stride behind the drums. We were all sad to see him go.

My friend, Celia Chambers (of Jon Martyn fame) who had a thing about drummers, had joined my wife to watch the band one Saturday evening. As is sometimes the case with attractive ladies who appear to be on their own, a strange man squeezed into the seat at their table, smiling and trying to catch their eye. Celia and Jane, however, were well-practised at ignoring creeps at gigs. When the gig finished, he got up and talked to the band before leaving. I finished packing up and went over to the ladies.

"Wasn't it great to see Rob!" I said.

They looked puzzled. "Rob who?"

"Rob Hirons. He's over from France and came to see us."

Jane said, "I didn't see him. What a shame he didn't come over to say hello."

My turn to look puzzled, "He was sitting at your table all night."

Jane was horrified, "Oh my god. I didn't recognise him without any hair! He must have spent several evenings every week at our house, but I never

The King Ivory Band. L-R; Ian Rose, CJ, Bob Duesbury and Johnny Vincent

really got to see his face. I feel so embarrassed we ignored him."

There was a long, uncomfortable silence.

Celia said quietly, "Darling. You didn't shag him."

The King Ivory Band played anywhere, including some dreadful dives. At one pub in Bradford, there was only one customer in the place when we arrived and a fight started. We hadn't even set up our gear before the guy reached over the bar, grabbed the barmaid and they started punching each other. In retrospect, I now realise, we were wasting our time playing original songs to some audiences. They would have preferred the usual covers band playing the classics like Honkytonk Woman and All Right Now. Still, we persisted, be it pearls before swine. It was a fine band and Johnny Vincent put many hours work into refining my songs.

After playing a gig at the Harrogate Blues Bar, Bob told me he'd got cancer and his days were numbered. Sound man Rod Holt kindly offered to record a live album which we barely completed before Bob sadly died. His picture still hangs on the wall, stage left, in the Blues Bar.

The King Ivory Band. L-R; Phil Snell, Bob Duesbury,
Bill White, Johnny Vincent and CJ

89

Queen Enterprises

Paul Humberstone had a scrapbook full of photographs from our Art School days, including photographs of Freddie and Tim Staffell. He had taken photographs of the first Smile recording session and I had photographs I'd taken of Freddie and Tim on the final day at Art School because I was going to Canada and America and wouldn't see them for some time. I also had photographs of Richard Thompson, Paul, Freddie, Tim and me, posing with guitars and drums outside our basement student flat, 42B Addison Gardens. They really should put up a blue plaque.

That morning, before the photo session, Freddie and Tim had gone to a

Outside 42b. L-R; Richard Thompson, Paul Humberstone. Freddie Bulsara, Tim Staffell and CJ. Photo taken by JT Spragg. (With permission – Mark Hayward)

music shop and bought themselves Fender guitars. Tim bought a white Stratocaster and Freddie a white Telecaster, both with rosewood fingerboards. They brought along Richard, who'd previously played in 1984 and Wreckage, to play drums and the four of us had a jam session. When we'd finished jamming, we stepped outside into the small yard. Bert Sprag stood on the pavement above and took the pictures. Paul (who can't play a note incidentally) picked up an old acoustic and, standing in the doorway, did his very best Elvis impersonation.

Years later, Paul and I put our photographs in a Sotheby's sale but they didn't sell. As a result, we were contacted by Queen Enterprises and arranged to meet Brian so that he could see them. Frank Moses came with us and Brian answered the front door. It was good to see him after all that time during which he'd become a guitar god, a little more tastefully and elegantly attired than hitherto but still the same Brian. He immediately asked about Clive, commenting on what a wonderful artist he is.

Soon we were all sitting on the carpet in the first-floor office with the photographs strewn all around us. It had only been five years since Freddie had died so Brian got quite nostalgic; he started telling us about his divorce and I found myself feeling rather sorry for him. Then I remembered he had several millions in the bank and I'd had trouble scraping together the money for the trip down to London. Paul told him, "You could always join Chris's band if you're looking for something to do. Of course, you'd have to play rhythm guitar at first but I reckon, after a few gigs, they'd gave you a couple of lead breaks."

We asked after Roger; Brian replied that he was on his boat. Paul, always the cheeky northerner asked, "Is it on the Norfolk Broads?"

Following our meeting, Brian was about to set off to take part in an event to celebrate the long career of Hank Marvin and the Shadows. I said, "When I had my Shadows band, I was happy if I could just manage to play the right notes. When you had your Shadows band, I'll bet you were particular about getting the reverb and echo just right." He said, "I was actually".

We agreed it was Hank's touch that was so magical to us as teenagers, using a wide variety of guitar tones and special effects. Hank was amazingly innovative.

A couple of weeks later, a letter arrived from Brian. I'd given him the tape of The King Ivory Band album and the recordings from the Paul Jones Show. He'd been playing them in his car and complemented Johnny Vince on his guitar playing as well as comparing two different versions of the song Shave and a Haircut -Two Bits. It was good to get his approval yet I don't think he realised it was me singing, after all, he only ever known me as an organist and harmony singer. I talked to Brian about the formation of Smile and he said "I've done three American tours, don't ask me to remember. Why don't you write this stuff down?" which was one of the ideas that prompted this book.

Back home, I was brought back to earth sitting in the pub next to Dave Holmes. A young woman came over and asked, "Didn't you used to be in a famous band?" I replied, "Yea, I was in Freddie and The Dreamers." Immediately Dave leaned over and said, "You've always been a Dreamer, Chris."

90

Smile Two

Tim Staffell and I decided to do some gigs together in London, which Tim organised. We recruited Clive to play bass and Tim's son, Andrew, to play drums, calling ourselves Smile Two. We did some original songs and the two of us sang close harmony on The Everly Brothers Dream, Dream, Dream. Tim sang Ain't No Sunshine When She's Gone by Bill Withers and we did some Buddy Holly songs too. I pointed out to the audience that we weren't sure what happened to the other two original members of Smile. I said the last we heard they were playing in a Queen tribute band; since then, as far as we know, they disappeared into obscurity. Later we did a gig in Otley at my local, the Junction, with Chill, (Mark Chillington) on drums.

Smile 2. L-R; Tim Staffell, CJ, Chill and Clive Armitage.

Chill had a Ska band called Little Chief and Ian Rose was their organist. Ian was unavailable so he asked me to cover for him. It was a complete departure for me. I rehearsed with the band and realised there were roughly five chords to each song be they in different keys. It wasn't rocket science; this was good time music. I set up at the back of the stage to the left of Chill with the bass player on his right. In front of us was a four-piece brass section with the guitarist, who was the singer, to their right. The audience stood before us, a sea of skinheads, all blokes, most of them in their thirties and forties, medication about to kick in, waiting in tense anticipation for us to begin.

THE HALFTONES, THE 12 BARS, THE SWINGING BROWN TROUSERS ? WHOEVER THEY WERE, ARE CAPTURED HERE ON THEIR ONE NITE EUROPEAN TOUR. STRUTTING AND PREENING IN KINGSTON AT THE GREY HOARSE. FAGS IN MOUTH, THEY DELIVERED A SALVO OF HITS FEW WOULD REMEMBER, MANY TRIED TO FORGET. HEARTS WERE BROKEN WITH AS MUCH REGULARITY AS THIER STRINGS. MY FOOTSTEPS ECHOED IN TIME WITH THE BASS AS I WALKED OUT OF THE EMPTYING ROOM TRYING TO REMEMBER WHERE I'D SEEN THE FAT ONE BEFORE.

SID BIGSBY N.M.E

Review by "Sid Bigsby" (aka Clive Armitage)

And we were off, the entire ageing skinhead crowd immediately started po-going, leaping frantically like they were still fifteen at a Madness gig, all arms and legs. It was an extraordinary sight.

Earlier that year, Jane and I had been in Paris when I'd spotted a graffiti wall where she took my photograph. Later, when we studied the picture, we realised it was the wall of Serge Gainsbourg's house. On a subsequent visit to London, staying the night at Tim Staffell's house in Richmond between recording sessions, I showed Tim the Paris photograph and the next morning he was up early working on his computer. He'd designed me an album cover and, with the words Positive Negative Space clearly emblazoned on the wall behind me, that became the album title.

It had been a lot of fun playing with Tim and he'd invited me to London to play keyboards on his album. Some weeks later, he told me Brian May ar-rived with his guitar tech and played on a new version of Tim's song, Earth. Brian turned up so loud they were concerned about disturbing the neigh-bours. Still, that's what rock n'roll is for.

Tim and me playing my local - The Junction- in Otley with Smile 2

Tim's design for my album cover – Positive Negative Space

Rehearsing in my kitchen

234

Smile 2 flyer

91

My Kind of Town

We'd known each other a couple of years. I remember it was 1997 because it was a year later that Jane and I were married. She was going to a medical conference in Chicago and I wasn't going to miss out on the chance of going with her. Chicago was the town where Muddy Waters had arrived by train in 1943 and started the definitive electric blues band with his friend Jimmy Rogers on guitar. Here they'd played house parties and worked in the factories when they first arrived from the south. Chicago was the town where the Stones had gone in 1964; at Chess Studios, 2020 South Michigan Avenue they'd recorded their Five by Five EP and several other hits.

There were three things I loved about Chicago; it was the home of the blues of course, I loved the architecture, both modern and stretching back to the nineteenth century and, finally, just off State Street (that great street) I discovered The Al Capone Museum. The museum was in the round and the audience stood in the centre. Scenes from Al's colourful, gangster life were then enacted mechanically all around us. There would be a gun-fight on a fire- escape and the next moment you turned around to the sound of police sirens and there'd be a car chase. Capone's actual office, along with his desk, had been brought from his very imposing sky-scraper building in the city and reconstructed in the museum. Behind the desk sat an automaton of Al himself, his head and hand moving back and forth as he smoked a cigar. It was classic 1950's - pure Ray Bradbury. It's sadly gone now; it should have had a preservation order on it.

I'd read in the local guide that Jimmy Rogers was playing that night at Buddy Guy's club, Legends. When I was a teenager and I bought my first blues compilation album, there was a track, The World is in a Tangle by Jimmy Rogers. I thought, from the way he sang, that he must be a white guy, but I was wrong; I later learned he was Muddy's guitarist.

Arriving at Legends, we took our seats on the second row by the stage. On the front row to our right sat Buddy Guy and next to him the man himself, Jimmy Rogers. He soon joined the band on stage. He was dressed in a brown chalk- striped suit and a brown trilby hat. Apart from being an old guy, he was dressed like he'd just stepped down off of the train when he'd first arrived in the forties. Later I learned it must have been one of his last concerts because he died shortly afterwards.

Another night we found a dark and smoky blues club where a black guy in his fifties was singing and playing great blues guitar with a younger generation band of funk musicians. I thought that combination was really interesting. He was performing classic blues and soul numbers including Midnight Hour. He turned out to be Jimmy Johnson. The next day I bought his album, recorded on Chicago's prestigious blues record label, Alligator Records,

Chicago is like a chess board, poor black areas right next to affluent white areas, with designer shops and swanky hotels. I wandered down a side street off Michigan Avenue one afternoon and found a thrift shop, a second -hand store. In the widow were various musical instruments including a couple of guitars that caught my interest so I ventured inside. It was like a scene from The Pawnbroker with Rod Steiger sitting behind the metal grill. He said, "You shouldn't be in here, white boy." (I was in my late forties at the time.) "You take a left and head back up that alley if you know what's good for you." I didn't argue. It seemed like something bad had just happened in there or was about to happen. I reminded myself, this was Chicago. You realise, anything that happens to you in America, good or bad, could be straight out of a film.

On State Street, I found Ray's Music, the music shop that had featured in The Blues Brothers. Everything was as it had been in the film, including the harmonicas that Elwood had checked out, still in that same case.

I bought a pair of shoes from a cheap shoe-shop, the kind of cool shoes you couldn't find in England. Later, back in England I was inspired to write a song called Blues Shoes, with the opening line "I bought these shoes on State Street in Chicago."

Jane would be at the conference most of the time but I spent the days wandering around on my own. I walked the back alleys, marvelling at the old buildings, taking pictures, soaking up the atmosphere. There are not many cities where I feel I could live, but Chicago is one of them.

92

Trying to Knock the Corners Off the Square

Religiously, every year, when The Magic Band came to the Irish Centre in Leeds, Richard Bostock and I would be there, as would Big Kev. We'd look forward to the finale, which was always, thankfully, Big Eyed Beans from Venus.

Every Wednesday lunchtime, for a couple of years, Richard Bostock, Andy Moss and myself would meet up at the Regent pub in Chapel Allerton and then head down to Richard's cellar in Chapeltown. It was a mess with equipment piled up, ashtrays overflowing with cigarette butts, instruments everywhere and yet it was an oasis, a little bit of heaven in troubled times. I'd always been interested in playing some music with a jazz attitude, which both Richard and Andy shared. I don't consider myself a jazz musician for a minute but the common ground we all shared was the blues. We also shared a love of a somewhat radical approach, the likes of Captain Beefheart and Charlie Mingus.

Each week I'd try to bring along a new song and they'd join in, not knowing any of the changes. The only clue was what key we were in. It was a Kind of Blue approach, where Miles Davis had been attempting to capture lightening in a bottle; the first take is there in the moment and has more spontaneity if you're really listening to each other. It takes total concentration and a little bit of luck. Of course, it doesn't always come off but it's always worth trying because it can be pure magic when it does work.

Over the months we learned to anticipate each other's playing and Richard would record everything on the primitive equipment he'd cobbled together. He got my vocals sounding better than top London studios where I'd previously recorded. I think that's because, as he got to understand the frequencies of my voice, he was able to tweak things. He would spend time during the week editing the sessions and eventually we compiled an album, including some cover versions, containing a dozen songs, warts and all. Sometimes I would play guitar and overdub keyboards - or the other way around - occasionally with harmonica. Richard would play double-bass and then overdub his saxophone when required. Andy's drumming was erratic and unorthodox, very much like Andy himself. Richard and I considered his approach unique, exciting and full of tension with dangerous corners that were not always navigable. We genuinely thought he had a touch of genius.

Dodger Harrison now lived in Brighton but, on his travels north, would occasionally meet us at the Regent and join in the sessions. It proved a creative time for me and I wrote a lot of songs. The Reverend Gary Davis said "I don't write no songs, they are revealed to me." There's a lot of truth in that, it's always the best way, when inspiration comes and the songs are revealed to you.

In Richard's cellar. L -R; Richard Bostock, CJ, Andy Moss

93

DT Blues

My friend DT was living in London and every Tuesday night his pal would bring his drumkit round to the flat. DT would play guitar or bass and they would jam late into the evening. One Tuesday there was a knock on the door; they immediately assumed it must be the neighbours coming round to complain. It was the neighbours; two guys from downstairs, father and son, but there was no complaint. In fact, quite the opposite. The neighbours said how much they'd been enjoying the music and asked if there was any chance, they might come along the following Tuesday and join in.

The next Tuesday, the neighbours, Alex and Nick, arrived with guitars, a bottle of brandy and some high-quality marijuana. Alex (the father) was the absolute epitome of cool. He spoke in a rich, plummy baritone and seemed to know a lot about American blues and roots music. Both father and son were accomplished players. As you might expect, a fine evening was had by all and along with much jollity, arrangements were made for the neighbours to return the following week. This continued for some weeks, Alex and Nick always turning up with a bottle of something rather special, along with enough top- quality marihuana to stun a rhino.

Some months later, DT was lying in his tent at a major music festival when he thought he heard a familiar voice, a field away, introducing Long John Baldry. DT shot out of the tent and, finding his way through the crowd, headed for the stage. By the time he arrived near the stage the announcer was introducing one of the Rolling Stones and DT was astonished to find that the man on the mic was none other than his neighbour, Alex, from their regular Tuesday night soiree. DT turned to a guy standing next to him in the crowd and said, "That's my neighbour up there on the stage."

The guy looked at him incredulously, "That's Alexis Korner, mate."

94

Anderson

When I told my friend Ronnie Brown I was adopted, he said, "I always wanted to be adopted."

I was born at St Mary's Hospital in Leeds. My mother, Deirdre Anderson, gave me up for adoption. She was twenty two years old; returning to Northern Ireland as an unmarried mother was not an option. The name I found on my birth certificate was Colin Anderson. There is no mention of my father. I was adopted through the Church of England Adoption Society by Tom and Ethel Smith and brought up in Leeds.

The district nurse paid us a visit from time to time. She let slip that Deirdre was herself a nurse and an Irish girl from Belfast. She had requested a photograph of me but was told it was not advisable.

My dad, Tom, died in 1985 and my adoptive mother, Ethel, in 2002. Tom would have understood and gladly welcomed my seeking my birth family, but I felt Ethel was not equipped to deal with such an event. Later in 2002, now feeling more assured and having the support of my wife, Jane, we pursued finding my birth family. My records had been mysteriously burned in a fire (apparently a common occurrence where adoption records are concerned). We contacted a genealogist in Carrick Fergus who found Deirdre within days. She had been living in a nursing home in Bangor and, through an adoption councillor in Leeds, a letter was sent. Unfortunately, Deirdre had recently died (about the same time as Ethel) so the letter was passed on to my sister, Sandra. Talk about luck of the Irish, she was the only person who knew about me. She had been sworn to secrecy at the age of seventeen when her first daughter, Karen, was born. Even my brother, Adrian, knew nothing of me. After counselling, letters were exchanged and eventually I met my entire family within twenty- four hours.

Musician Paul Buckley lives in Donegall and he gave me a lift. We caught the ferry over to Belfast and he dropped me off alone, at the end of my sister's street. My knees were knocking by the time I reached Sandra's house. Her husband Norman answered the door, took one look at me and in a broad Belfast accent exclaimed, "Oh. My. God!" To him, the family resemblance was obvious. I'd never met anyone who looked like me apart from my daughters. Can you imagine - here's another person who looks like you and here comes another. If you put Sandra's daughters and my daughters together, they look like peas in a pod. It was a wonderful yet overwhelming experience.

They were a lovely, unpretentious and very ordinary Irish family and so welcoming. They threw a big party for me and the next day, we all ended up sitting around a table having a meal at the Marine Hotel in Bangor. I felt an instant connection as if the earth wire had been attached. It was a profound moment to suddenly realise that I belonged. Not to know who you are is a terrible thing and caused me to go off the rails for far too many years. It undermines your confidence and you recognise that other people have a certain assurance that you don't have. It's made a huge difference to me personally to find my family and, as Jackson Browne put it, "To finally arrive in the world."[1]

It seems like Deirdre met my father in England so the chances are, I'm half- Irish. I'm Irish from the waist down (like the man who invented Irish dancing).

When I told my friend, Derek Lawrenson, I'd discovered I was Irish. He said, "That accounts for everything."

95

Patrick and the Harp

My first teaching job was at a Young Offenders' prison and, as teaching goes, it was in at the deep end. Originally, I taught a music evening class once a week and eventually I was teaching art and music during the day, several days a week. Teaching eight young offenders can be like continuously spinning plates whilst riding a roller coaster. You need eyes in the back of your head together with a superhuman ability to anticipate any pranks they might get up to. These are not usually malicious, more for their own entertainment and to get one up on authority.

Patrick had no musical talent whatsoever, none at all, yet he was very appreciative if anyone, myself included, played something he liked. He was an enthusiastic cheer-leader, so I kept him on the class because he was fun and was good for morale. He was a fat lad who looked like Billy Bunter, and I imagined he was the one who got caught because he couldn't run fast enough, while his mates got away. With his big owl face and little round glasses, Patrick would unload pencils, music books, anything he could lay his hands on, onto my desk at the end of the lesson. "I'm sorry," he'd say "I can't help it, I'm a kleptomaniac."

Over the weeks it became a standing joke, with him eventually pulling a keyboard from within his copious baggy trousers, to howls of laughter from everyone. As they left the class the lads would be searched, patted down by the screws. Patrick was so proficient at concealing stuff about his ample person that, unknown to any of the staff, he was amassing quite an arsenal of office supplies, secreted in his pad (his cell).

I was a little naïve, I suppose, when he suggested I might give him a harmonica. I'd only been there a few months and it seemed like a reasonable request. Giving prisoners anything at all was strictly forbidden, but I was still green. Anyway, I had an old harmonica with a couple of notes missing. What could possibly go wrong? So, unwittingly, I gave Patrick the harp and he managed to keep the entire cell block awake half the night playing the damned thing, with the result that they searched his pad. They found so much contraband, you'd think he was running a small tool shop and stationery business. To my intense relief he never squealed about where he got the harmonica.

Johnny Vincent, since his return from London, had worked his way up to head gardener on the Council and, recently, he'd assumed an executive position. I had a word with him about Patrick. Patrick was a local lad so I wondered if Johnny could find him a little job on the parks, using his influence and a word in the right ear. I told Patrick my idea and he dismissed it saying, "I don't need a job, I've got loads of money," which puzzled me. I was intrigued, so much so that I did something unprecedented; I looked up his file to find out what crime he'd committed. It transpired that he lay in wait at motorway services to steal car transporters loaded with new cars, which he would then drive to the Continent. There he'd pick up massive amounts of money in exchange for the cars. The money would then be deposited in his Swiss bank accounts, of which he had several. I had clearly underestimated his considerable talents, not to say his sheer nerve. Henceforth I looked at Patrick through new eyes, (making sure I never gave him any more musical instruments.)

96

The Lightnin' Sessions

The first time I saw the Who in 1965, the support group was The Outer Limits. Their front man, Jeff Christie, was standing up playing an unusually short keyboard on tall legs. Later, under his own name, he had a big hit record with Yellow River. I was also impressed by The Outer Limits guitarist, a skinny little guy called Steve Isherwood. A couple of years later, in '67, Steve joined the Hogline on trumpet. Steve had just been on the Jimi Hendrix Tour with The Outer Limits.

In the nineties, I played keyboards for Midnight Train for a short time after their keyboard player left. I'd known their singer, Grom Kelly, since '67, when I first met him back at the Hole in the Wall in Bradford. Now, my oldest friend Duffy was on bass and Steve played guitar. Though a formidable guitar player, Steve was stoned a lot of the time. Ok, most musicians I know smoked dope from time to time but Steve smoked industrial quantities and consequently was not always on the razor's edge. He also spoke very slowly and deliberately and Duffy, with his propensity for nicknames, named him Lightnin'.

One Friday night, on our way to a gig, we called to collect Steve from his first- floor flat in Headingly. Duffy rang the bell and we waited on the doorstep for what seemed like an eternity. Eventually we heard footsteps coming down the stairs, along the hall and, finally, Steve answered the door. He was wearing his dressing gown and carpet slippers and smoking the biggest conical spliff you've ever seen. He looked rather puzzled and much to our amusement announced, "I thought it was Wednesday."

Years later, when I formed the first C.J.Smith Band, Steve joined, along with Ian Rose. We had Chuck McLaughlin on bass and Eddie Sparrow on drums. Chuck was from Denver Colorado and would later become the Wolves' bassman.

As a teenager in the early sixties, Eddie Sparrow had gone to London and wound up at the Two Eyes Coffee Bar where he became friends with guitarist Albert Lee. The Beatles were doing an audition in London and were sleeping in their van just around the corner from Eddie's flat, so Eddie's landlord arranged for them to stay with Eddie for a few days. Sometime later, Eddie moved to Hamburg where he played drums in Tony Sheridan's band, after Ringo Star had left. He also played jazz in Paris for a while. Eddie Sparrow's got some stories to tell.

In Steve's basement, with this line-up, we recorded an album. For the few tracks when Eddie wasn't available, Steve programmed the drums. For a non - drummer he did a remarkable job. Steve would become obsessed with the finer details when it came to mixing the tracks. They turned out well but eventually you had to say to Steve, "Take your hands off the controls and step away from the mixing desk."

We called the album "The Lightnin' Sessions.

97

Shave 'n' a Haircut – Two Bits

W hen The King Ivory Band arrived at Pebble Mill Studios in Birmingham, we were met by two BBC technicians in brown dust coats. They helped us unload our equipment onto two large trolleys, said, "Leave everything to us," and directed us to the bar. When guitarist, Johnny Vincent, decided he'd had exactly the correct amount of beer, we made our way to the studio. It was one of those big BBC studios like Abbey Road; the control room was up a flight of stairs so the producer could look down and see all the musicians.

This was 1996 and my friend, Kevin Thorpe, had recently recorded a session there for the Paul Jones Show with his band, Out of the Blue. He'd given a copy of the King Ivory Band's first album to the producer, who'd then booked us for the show. Down in the studio, our equipment was already set in place with screens around each instrument. My electric piano was set up next to the grand piano. We recorded our first song. The producer was happy with the result so we recorded three more songs. They were all first or second takes, recorded live, just like they did in the old days, ready for the show the following week.

The last song we recorded was Shave and a Haircut – Two Bits. It was a collection of stories I'd put together, about the second Sonny Boy Williamson, real name Rice Miller. When I returned to the control room, the producer said, "I want you to go back down there and talk it instead of singing it." He wanted me to do a rap but in my own voice. After re-recording the vocal, I immediately knew it had worked because our drummer, Bill White, was sitting there with his thumb in his mouth, like a kid who'd just been read his favourite bedtime story. I realised these BBC guys don't just have technical knowledge and great ears, they're full of imaginative ideas too. When our songs were played on the show, people started to take notice and some of our friends started to take our music a little more seriously.

Grom Kelly showed me a harmonica Sonny Boy had given him back in the day. Andy Moss also met Sonny Boy, and the last verse is Andy's story.

Shave 'n' a Haircut – Two Bits

In 1964, Sonny Boy Williamson made a tour of the UK.
He was most impressed by the pin-striped suit of the London city businessman.
So, carrying a rolled umbrella, he wore kid gloves and a bowler hat 'N' a two-
tone suit in alternating panels of grey and charcoal grey.
An unusual choice, considering the style of the day.

They say he was a genius I don't know but he could make that harmonica weep.
I bought his records and I dug his music and the funny way he used to speak.
Legend has it that he was mean and ornery and that he did drink a bit so When
he returned home, folks did not believe that in England he'd become a hit.

I saw him blowing his harp in his dressing room one night back in '64.
There was a Bo Diddley record playing out there in the hall.
He said, "Hey, do y'hear that beat? I knew some day that'd be a hit.
Why, we used to call that Shave 'n' a Haircut – Two Bits

'See it goes, Shave 'n' a Haircut – Two Bits. Y'dig it?
It goes Shave 'n' a Haircut – Two Bits"
Shave 'n' a Haircut – Shave 'n' a Haircut – Two Bits – Two Bits.

98

A Piece of Cake

In 2011 at a local festival, Lindley Woodstock, I was introduced to guitarist, Tim Lyttle, by his wife, the folk singer Patsy Matheson. We discovered we both loved Albert King's music and he invited me along to sing with his funk band, as their lead singer had just left. I turned up with my Stratocaster and immediately realised that Tim had a fantastic rhythm section in Rich Ferdinando and Nick Earny and was a damned funky blues guitarist himself. What they needed was a Hammond organ. Mine had been broken for two years (as I'd stupidly let a drunk friend carry it to my car after a gig and he'd dropped it). I phoned Hammond U.K. and they offered me four hundred quid for the broken Ham-

Wolves gig with Chris Campbell at The Lantern, Halifax

mond in part exchange for the new XK1.

Perhaps subconsciously I was thinking of Peter and the Wolves, I don't know but in 2012 we named the band The Wolves. We sent our first album to the Paul Jones Show, which broadcast on Monday nights on radio 2. I'd been teaching guitar at the Army Foundation College on Penny Pot Lane in Harrogate and, at the end of my evening class, returned to my car and started up the engine. Immediately I heard the title track of The Wolves album, A Piece of Cake. I assumed I'd left the CD in the player but when I opened it there was no CD. When the song ended Paul Jones said, "I really liked that." Hey, The Wolves were on the radio.

Rich, our drummer, lives on a canal boat on the Leeds and Liverpool canal. He was working on his boat, half listening to the Paul Jones Show, when he suddenly thought; that drummer plays a lot like me......... Oh, it is me! I drove home calling at Tim's; everyone had phoned each other by that time and celebrations were in order. It's a big thing when you first hear your song played on the radio and at that moment, for these guys, it was a major achievement. The reason we called the first Wolves album "A Piece of Cake" was because I made a cake each week and we never had a Wolves rehearsal without it. (Our days of whiskey and drugs were long over.) They commissioned me to write the song so I started thinking, life could be a piece of cake

The Wolves with the Wolf

but it isn't. So, then the song wrote itself.

Stonking Steve became our biggest fan. We called him Stonking because he would unfailingly approach us at the end of a gig exclaiming, "That was stonking!" On arrival at a gig, he would greet us with, "It's so good to see your happy smiling faces," in his broad Yorkshire accent. To look at him, it would be easy to come to the conclusion that he's not anything like as smart as he is. He would regularly go around the audience selling our CDs, with an irresistible sales pitch, often achieving unprecedented results. Following a gig, he would always offer to help us out with our gear. One evening, after playing the Harrogate Blues Bar, he carried one of my heavy Mackie PA speakers to my car, depositing the bulky speaker next to me on the passenger seat. Passing the seat-belt around the speaker, he handed it to me to fasten and make secure. He looked thoughtful, "I've fastened women into my car who look worse than this." He went on, "But I say, in the middle of winter, it doesn't matter what they look like, as long as you've something warm to cuddle up to."

Nick Earny soon found it difficult to find time for rehearsals so we brought in my American friend Chuck McLaughlin on bass. Chuck has quite a collection of basses including a Gibson Ripper, a Fender Fiftieth Anniversary Precision, a Dan Electro Longhorn bass, not to mention his collection

The Wolves' American bass-man, Chuck McLaughlin

of electric guitars, including a Roger McGuinn twelve-string Rickenbacker which he'd lend me occasionally. He is a formidable bass player and is accomplished in so many styles. I once asked him how come he could play just about any genre of music. He told me, in America you might be playing in a western swing band one night, the next night you're playing jazz, next night pop, next night you're playing blues at a jam-session, so you learn it all. Chuck's job meant he eventually had to return to Aspin, Colorado, where he's now the go-to bass player in town. We were sad to see him go. He's a very sweet, quietly spoken bear of a man who is able to stand perfectly still on stage, with only his fingers moving, and tear the house down. He comes across the pond from time to time and on his last visit we played Harrogate Blues Bar with him. After one short rehearsal Chuck remembered everything, played like he'd never left.

For our next bass player, we recruited James Heggie, who played with Rich in his other band, Crosscut Saw. James played on the second Wolves album and, being a talented graphic designer, he designed a splendid cover. We were delighted to get some royalties which paid for the album.

James unfortunately moved out of town and Tim and I wondered if we could stand to go through the process of having to rehearse yet another bass player. I rang Chris Campbell, lead guitarist with the Reggie band, Mojah, to ask him if he knew the whereabouts of a bass player called Hamlet, who I'd worked with in the eighties in Chapeltown. Chris knew Hamlet but he said he fancied having a go himself. I didn't know he played the bass; he played lead guitar for Finley Quayle for years and travelled the world before returning to Chapeltown. I'd grown friendly with him when I'd seen him play in Mojah, with his partner, Paulette and her sister Annette. We'd played together in Exiles Intact, and they'd recently sung on The Wolves' album. Chris fit right in, a phenomenal musician, he brought a new positive vibe to the band and he's a big personality. When we'd leave, we'd always say, "One Love" to each other and it's a beautiful thing.

Chris and Rich locked right in. A major problem was that Rich lives so far away and rehearsals became difficult to organise. I could see Tim was having difficulties juggling the band and his job, finding time generally became too much of a problem. It became frustrating and eventually I started the C.J.Smith Band as an outlet for my writing and to establish a broader musical scope.

One essential thing with bands is that it works best if you all live in the same vicinity, (unless of course you all have the technology to rehearse and record on line). Bands have a life of their own and it was time to close it down for a while. Hopefully when the mojo returns, we'll reform because I miss playing with those guys and I love them dearly. As Neil Young pointed out; you've got to follow the muse wherever it takes you and sometimes that can be hard on people and hard on yourself too. Leave the field fallow for a while and hopefully in time it will produce a better crop.

One Love.

My drawing of Harrogate Blues Bar

99

Days of Our Lives

I got a phone call from Matt, the director, to say they were making a new Queen film about Freddie's life and asking me to take part. We discussed various locations and he suggested Ealing College as a likely place. I told him the Art School was gone and it was just like any polytechnic now, the vibe wouldn't be there. I suggested the rehearsal room at Imperial, where Brian had put the advert for a drummer, which Roger had answered, and where Smile had our first rehearsals. I'd always referred to it as the Broom Cupboard. It wasn't that small but it was where they stored the kettle drums so there wasn't too much room to rehearse. He liked that idea but didn't mention it again. On subsequent phone calls, we finally agreed that I would meet them at lunchtime at the West Kensington Pub on Elsham Road, where, in those college days, Smile, Freddie's band Wreckage, and our friends used to meet.

When I arrived, Matt, his sound man and camera man were already there setting up with lights and flight cases, wires everywhere. The pub was closed to the public so Matt suggested they take a break and we went across the road to a restaurant for lunch. I had a list of likely questions as did Matt. I'd already told him a lot of my story so he could pick out the questions he wanted to ask. We discussed this in more detail over lunch and then I got talking to the camera man. We discovered we were both Neil Young fans; he'd done a film with Neil at his ranch. Neil had given him access to a home movie of the Harvest band rehearsing in his barn, playing Words (between the Lines of Age.) A still from the home movie had been used for the back cover of Harvest and now, much to his delight, they were able to bring that back cover to life. I gave him my address and a week later a copy of the film arrived through my letterbox.

Back at the pub we started filming. I told Matt about meeting Freddie at Ealing, the Cowboy song, and I re-enacted "I'm going to be a Legend," all of which made the film, although much of our conversation would inevitably end up on the cutting room floor. When Matt asked me about Roger, I said, "I think it's fair to say, even before he was famous, Roger's life was a sexual

Disneyland." The film crew cracked up laughing and it had to be shot three times. Matt rang me a few days later; he'd showed it to all his mates (I'm not sure that included Brian and Roger, whom he was filming over those next few days). He said, "You know they're going to cut it don't you?"

"They can't cut that, it's my best line," I complained, They cut it.

The film opened with Brian being interviewed in the Broom Cupboard, talking about the first Smile rehearsal. Matt had put my broom cupboard idea to good use after all.

Sometime later, Matt phoned again. He was working for I.T.V on a programme, The 60 Greatest Hit Singles of All Time. Apparently, the producer had seen me in Days of Our Lives and said to Matt, "Let's get that guy to introduce Bohemian Rhapsody." I was rather hesitant, thinking it might be cheesy.

Matt was insistent, "Come on, you've got to do it, it'll be fine." It was filmed in a beautiful old theatre in Leicester Square, with a circular gallery.

I took Andy Davis along for moral support. He'd been editor of Record Collector and published a letter I'd written setting the record straight on a couple of points about the early days of Smile. Later I'd worked on a book of photographs he was editing called Queen on Camera, Off Guard.[1] The book included some of mine and Paul Humberstone's photographs which

With Tim Staffell at his local in Richmond Surrey 2019

we'd sold to the author.

I'd given Andy a copy of one of my albums which he assumed was heavy northern blues/ Gary Moore style. When he finally got round to playing it, he rang me to tell me my songs were the best things he'd heard in a long time and admitted that he'd ended up in floods of tears. He offered to help me and organised a photographer friend to do a photo shoot on Eel Pie Island. Then together, they redesigned the album cover, Andy wrote the liner notes, and we rejigged the tracks. They did a professional job and I'm very grateful to them.

When I arrived at the theatre with Andy, there was a grand piano on the stage surrounded by lights and cameras. That day they were shooting just the piano players. (The guy before me was Mick Gallagher, the piano player from the Blockheads, Ian Dury's band.)

I'd re-learned the Cowboy song, practising crossing my hands, Freddie-style. They only wanted the first couple of lines so they could cut from me singing it to Freddie performing the song with Queen. When it was televised, I watched with mounting anticipation as we got to the final ten, and then to the concluding announcement of Bohemian Rhapsody.

Suddenly I'm transported back to the Broom Cupboard where Brian is playing a new song he's just written. He's showing us the chord sequence and we're adding harmonies for the hook line that goes, "Is this the real life."

Then I'm in the music department at Ealing. It's 1968 and Freddie is sitting there with his head in his hands asking "Why are we so crap? Why can't we write a decent song like Tim and Brian?"

Then it's a week later, I'm sitting at the piano looking over my shoulder at Freddie, standing there in his white Levi jacket. I'm saying, "After the link, we go into the Cowboy Song and then I'm not sure which bit to use next. What do you think?" Freddie's saying, "Well move over, Rover, and let Freddie take over."

Before I know it, it's seven years later, 1975 and I'm watching Top of the Pops. The video with the new Queen single is playing. My first thought is," Oh, he's finished the song."

All of these images rush before me as I'm about to introduce The Greatest Hit Single of All Time. I don't know this cartoon comic-book hero Freddie Mercury and yet my overwhelming feeling at this moment is, I sure miss my friend Freddie Bulsara.

Then I remember the last thing he said to me - Good Luck.

The Epilogue or
The News in Welsh

I always imagined that, someday, I'd become an old bluesman and have a blues-based band that would combine all the influences and styles of music I'd picked up along the way. At last, I'm fulfilling that dream. It's nothing to do with fame and fortune, it's about creativity and the adventure that music has always been for me. Of course, it would have been great to have had the confidence and experience to have done this in my early twenties, like some of my contemporaries, but for most musicians there are ways to go that we didn't always expect. As John Lennon said, "Life is what happens while you're making other plans." Looking back, I only wish I'd focussed on the positive in each situation and lived in the moment, instead of fretting about the past or worrying excessively about the future because that way, we'd enjoy life more.

I'm lucky to have had a such a rich musical life and finally to have found a band who are all on the same page and enjoy working on my songs. Ian Rose was the foundation of the C.J.Smith Band for me. We'd played together in the King Ivory Band so with Ian on Hammond and me on piano, we have that gospel combination that I love and we never seem to get in each other's way. Ian brought along his friend, John Heap. The two of them are a double act, both hilariously funny guys, and they've been in bands together since they were teenagers. John is a fine bass player, one of the best. His other great strength in this band is that he thinks like an arranger. I come up with a song and he immediately hones in on the groove and begins mapping out the possibilities of an arrangement. Along with our drummer, John Shepard, the rhythm section has become the beating heart of the band.

John Shepard played in Acoustic Alchemy in the States for years. He started as their drum tech and when their drummer joined Lyle Lovett's band, John landed the job. He played stadiums all over America. Previously John was A&R man (artists and repertoire) for Phonogram Records and originally signed Def Leppard. They told him they had offers from other companies but John told them that he'd get a hundred quid bonus if he signed them and that he really needed the money to buy a new stair carpet. That clinched the deal.

To complete the band, we were lucky enough to recruit our youngest member and one of the finest blues guitarists in Leeds, Christy Herron. Christy fronts his own band, The Christy Herron Band, playing twelve bar classics. I've sat in on several occasions when his keyboard player has been unavailable. Christy told me he'd like to branch out into something a little more challenging, so I invited him along. With his refinement and skill as a guitarist, along with Ian Rose, we now have two accomplished lead players - virtuosos we can feature. When I started out, the queue for the guitarist's job was right down the street and around the block so luckily, I learned to play keyboards, thanks again to my first piano teacher, Mr Alway. Occasionally, when Christy is unavailable, Johnny Vincent joins the band and it's like he's always been there. Having a recognisable sound, I can bring in all the influences and styles acquired over the years and we can make our own stew

Poster design - John Shepard

out of it. It's something I've been wanting to do since I heard The Band back in the late sixties.

Looking back, you realise what momentous times my generation have lived through. In the history of humanity, it was undoubtedly the best time to be alive. Born after the second world war, Clement Attlee's Labour government introduced the Welfare State and the National Health Service, even though the cupboard was bare. We were lucky and naively imagined that things would always continue to get better. It wasn't to be.

I've been writing this book in lockdown, in the time of corona virus. It was also an ideal opportunity to write a bunch of songs as well and paint and draw and make cakes. Like a lot of folks in this difficult time, I've tried to keep creative in order not to go stir-crazy. Writing about the ups and downs of my musical life has been both therapeutic and stimulating. I have these

My painting for John's bass-drum (logo design - John Shepard)

snap-shots in my mind and as I've recalled them, it's triggered more recollections. I hope these stories have been as much fun for you to read, as they have been for me to recall.

In his song Mississippi, [1] Dylan sang, "I've got nothing but affection for those who sailed with me," which I hope conveys the spirit of this book.

If you would like to hear the CJ Smith Band:

Retrospective 1995-2010 by C.J. Smith on Amazon Music - Amazon.com

https://open.spotify.com/album/1XJd54b5QfKgBZE5Hqi8IV

All songs\ lyrics by CJ Smith Copyright Widesmile Music

https://open.spotify.com/album/0wLBh80iIjXM23icLXXRk7?si=Yyx2NYk
ZTUy0inb94VruuQ&utm_source=native-share-menu

Widesmile Music logo design – River Six

Acknowledgements

Thanks to The Courthouse Writers (especially Steph Shields and Brenda Cromwell) for their belief and encouragement for my first drafts; to my wife, Jane, for editing and grammar-bullying; to Meuryn Hughes at Aureus for his faith in my project.

References

Chapter 4
1. Roots, Radicals and Rockers, How Skiffle Changed the World, Billy
   Bragg: Faber & Faber, 2017,

Chapter 7
1. I Saw Her Standing There, (Song), Lennon & McCartney: Parlophone,
   1963
2. Chronicles, Dylan: Simon & Schuster, 2004
3. The Wild One, (Film), Stanley Kramer:1953

Chapter 10
1. The Clapping Song, (Song), Lincoln Chase, 1965
2. You Really Got Me: (Song), Davies, 1964

Chapter 11
1. Beatles Gear, Babiuk: Backbeat Books/Outline Press, 2001

Chapter 18
1. She Belongs to Me, (Song), Dylan: CBS records, 1964

Chapter 24
1. My Girl, (Song), White & Robinson: EMI Blackwood Music Inc, 1965
2. The Times They Are A-Changing, (Song), Dylan: CBS Records 1963

Chapter 25
1. Rosalyn, (Song), Duncan & Farley: Fontana Records, 1964

Chapter 29
1. Little Wing, (Song), Hendrix: Track Record, 1967

Chapter 36
1. Honey Pie, (Song), Lennon-McCartney: Apple, 1968

Chapter 39
1. You can't always get what you want, (Song), Jagger- Richards: Decca, 1969

Chapter 40
1. Sgt Pepper's Lonely Hearts Club Band (song) Lennon-McCartney: Parlophone. 1967

Chapter 42
1. Bohemian Rhapsody, (Song), Mercury: EMI, 1975
2. A Day in the Life, (Song), Lennon-McCartney: Parlophone. 1967

Chapter 46
1. Star, Star, (Song), Jagger/Richards: Rolling Stones/Virgin. 1973 Chapter

Chapter 47
1. You Never Give me your Money, (Song), Lennon-McCartney: Apple. 1969

Chapter 48
1. Feats Don't Fail Me Now, (Song), Barrère, George, Martin Kibbee: Warner Bros, 1974
2. Born to Run, (Song), Springsteen: CBS, 1975

Chapter 49
1. You Can't Catch Me, (Song), Berry: Chess, 1956
2. America, (Song), Simon: CBS, 1968

Chapter 51
1. In a Station, (Song), Manuel: CBS, 1968

Chapter 53
1. Look At Me I'm Wonderful, (Song), Stanshall: Liberty, 1969

Chapter 54
1. Sir Henry at Rawlinson End, (Album), Stanshall: Charisma Records 1978

Chapter 55
1. Tonight's the Night, (Song), Young: Reprise Records, 1975
2. Stephen Stills (solo album): Atlantic Records: 1970

Chapter 57
2. Big Yellow Taxi, (Song), Mitchell: Reprise Records: 1970

Chapter 58
1. A Spaniard in the Works, (Book), Lennon: Jonathan Cape, 1965

Chapter 61
1. Killer Queen, (Song), Mercury: EMI,1974

Chapter 67
1. Jumblequeen, (Song), St John: Chrysalis: 1974

Chapter 70
1. Adam Raised a Cain, (Song), Springsteen: CBS, 1978

Chapter 71
1. Sam with the Showing Scalp Flat-Top, (Song), Van Vliet: Beefheart
   Music, 1973
2. Common Sense, (Song), Prine: Atlantic Records, 1975

Chapter 82
1. Move it on Over, (Song), Williams: MGM,1947

Chapter 83
1. Riot in Cell Block Number 9 (Song), Lieber & Stoller: Spark Records,
   1954

Chapter 85
1. Kung Fu Fighting (Song), Douglas: Pye, 1974

Chapter 94
1. Alive in the World (Song), Browne: Elektra Records, 1996

Chapter 99
1. Queen on Camera Off Guard (Book), Hayward: Pavilion: 2011 Epilogue

Epilogue or The News in Welsh
1. Mississippi (Song), Dylan: CBS, 2001

Printed in Great Britain
by Amazon

19651012R10154